30 PRAYERS FOR MY UNBELIEVING SPOUSE

Warring for Their Soul While God Works on Yours

30 PRAYERS FOR MY UNBELIEVING SPOUSE

Warring for Their Soul While God Works on Yours

Capri Lee

yo PUBLISHING

30 Prayers For My Unbelieving Spouse by Capri Lee

ISBN: 979-8-9901758-8-4

Published in the United States by Yosi Publishing, LLC. For more inquiries or permissions, please contact the publisher at www.yosipublishing.com

Cover Design by Daria McFadgen

This book is not intended as a substitute for professional counseling or therapy. The author shares personal reflections and scriptural devotions for encouragement purposes only.

This book is dedicated to:

My cousin, Victor Young, Jr. — Thank you for seeing the writer in me long before I did. Back in 2008, you encouraged me to write a different book, and your belief in my potential never wavered, even when mine did.

Linda Clifford — In your final days, I truly believe you encountered the True and Living God. That hope brings me peace.

My husband — I believe that you will find the Truth, and that Truth will set you free.

Contents

Introduction

"But Jesus beheld them, and said unto them, With men this is impossible; but with God all things are possible." — Matthew 19:26 KJV

This devotional is for every blood-bought believer—whether you were saved before or after saying "I do"—who has cried out for God to change what seems "wrong" in your spouse. I get it. You picked up this book expecting prayers aimed at fixing your husband or wife. Sorry to disappoint you—but this book isn't about fixing them. It's about allowing God to do the deep, necessary work in us, so that we can love, live with, and lead our spouses with Christ at the helm, steering us in the right direction.

Yes, your spouse may be part of the problem. But let's be honest: they're not the only one. Sometimes, the issue isn't just their behavior—it's how we see them. Are we building them up, or always pointing out what they do wrong? Are we speaking life into our marriage or rehearsing defeat? Are we learning their love languages or just repeating how we want to be loved? Are we giving grace or being selfish, silent and spiteful? Do we play the part at church, only to come home and withhold the very love Christ commands?

If your spouse were asked about your character, what might they say? Do you think they would recognize these qualities in you?

When I reconnected with my now-husband in 2010—my high school sweetheart—I knew the kind of life he lived, and he knew mine. His father was the Minister of Music at the church where we met, so he knew church was my second home. But he still saw me as that teenage girl who used to sneak around the corner to kiss him during altar call (don't judge me). What he didn't know was that the girl he remembered had grown into a woman of God—bold, baptized, Holy Ghost-filled, and serious about her salvation. I had been transformed. Or so I thought.

I started to compromise my beliefs. I got too comfortable playing with fire that, after a while, the burns didn't bother me. I moved in with him and his family, and before long, I had backslidden. I still went to church—but not consistently. And the more time passed, the more his lifestyle came into focus. The things he now did, he eventually admitted were always a part of his life, even when we dated as kids. But I held on, telling myself that my love would change him. That my prayers would save him. That surely, he'd come to Christ...soon.

Twelve years of marriage and a baby later, we're still unequally yoked. Some days, I believe with all my heart that God will save him. Other days, I'm worn out and wondering if God hears me at all. I've fasted. I've cried. I've prayed prayers that began with "God, fix him!" and ended with "God, deliver him!" But it was in one of my most desperate moments—around 3 a.m., questioning God in the shower and asking for a resource to help those like me—that He whispered something unexpected: *"Write it."*

So here it is. A 30-day devotional. Not just for your spouse, but for *you.* For us. For the silent warriors who feel alone in a battle that others don't understand. This devotional is the encouragement I needed in the moments I wanted to give up. The answers I asked God for when I felt forgotten. This is as much my breakthrough as it will be yours.

What can you expect over the next 30 days? As my dad often says, "one thing's for sure and two thing's for certain"—this is not a book of prayers asking God to "get them" or even to "change them." This is about letting God work in *us.* Yes, He absolutely can save and transform your spouse—but what if He's using this very season to transform you first?

1 Corinthians 7:14 reminds us that our spouses are sanctified through us. That means the grace, mercy, and blessings flowing to us are also reaching them. And verse 16 asks us a powerful question: *What if your godly life becomes the spark for their salvation?* Are you willing to believe for that?

This book is about heart posture. About shifting our perspective. About allowing God to take our eyes off our spouse's flaws and fix them on Him. It's about inner work—healing our wounds, renewing our vision, refining our language. *The way we think about our spouses shapes what we say and how we pray.*

If you don't believe they can be saved, you'll stop praying like it. You'll stop speaking life over them. You'll unknowingly declare defeat over their future. This I know personally. But when God transforms your heart, He also transforms your vision. You begin to see your spouse through His eyes—eyes filled with compassion, mercy, and hope. Jesus didn't just die for the already righteous. He died for the lost, the broken, the bound including your spouse. And if He loved them enough to give His life, the least we can do is love them through this process.

When we love through Christ's eyes, our actions shift. We respond with grace, even in disappointment. We grow in patience in times of angst. We learn to listen and communicate clearly. We give space when needed. We serve them, not out of obligation, but out of obedience—even when it's hard.

And with changed actions come changed prayers. You'll stop praying for convenience and start interceding for *conversion*. You'll pray not just for a better marriage, but for a soul saved from destruction. Because that's what this is: spiritual warfare. The enemy is after the foundation of your family. If he can dismantle your marriage, he can damage generations. So yes, you'll find prayers here to break generational curses, petitions for God to fill the gaps with legacy-building blessings, encouragement when your hope runs dry, and insight when the answers seem hidden.

At the end of each day, take time to reflect. Journal what God reveals to you. Meditate on the scripture. Speak the prayer aloud. And just because it's written for 30 days doesn't mean you have to rush. Revisit the days that speak to you. Linger where God is working. This is a journey of detox and divine readjustment. A journey toward transformation, praying not just for a salvation in your spouse, but for a remodeling in *you*—one that brings healing, wholeness, and holy perspective.

One

What Is Marriage?

"Therefore shall a man leave his father and his mother, and shall cleave unto his wife: and they shall be one flesh." — Genesis 2:24 KJV

Marriage—what is it, really? Merriam-Webster defines marriage as an *intimate or close union; the state of being united as spouses in a consensual and contractual relationship recognized by law.* But in Genesis 2:21–23, God shows us something far deeper. Marriage is a holy *covenant*, divinely designed by a holy God. It's not just a union—it's a blood covenant, a sacred bond between a man and a woman, bound by purpose and blessed by God.

To truly grasp the weight of marriage, we must first understand what a covenant truly is. Dr. Tony Evans describes a covenant as a divinely created relational bond—a covering from God. Throughout Scripture, we see God entering covenant after covenant with His people, promising generational wealth, protection, land, prosperity, children, and more. And the most beautiful part? God always stands behind His covenants.

When God created the first marriage, He performed the first surgery. He caused Adam to fall into a deep sleep and took one of his ribs to form Eve. This act revealed something profound: though they were two individuals, they were still one flesh. Yet, within that oneness, there is still individuality. When Adam awoke and saw Eve, he didn't see a clone—he saw someone like him, yet distinct. She had parts he didn't have, a softness and beauty that was undeniably different. And in that moment, he recognized her uniqueness and gave her identity: *"This is now bone of my bone, flesh of my flesh. She shall be called woman, because she was taken out of man"* (Genesis 2:23 KJV). In naming her, he honored her identity. That moment wasn't just poetic—it was prophetic. Marriage requires unity and recognition of one another's distinct God-given purpose.

That act of bloodshed and binding is the foundation of marriage. It is not just a legal arrangement—it is a blood covenant. It is sacred. A divine agreement between one man and one woman, cleaving to one another as one flesh (*Mark 10:6–7 KJV*).

But what does it mean to *cleave*?

Let's go back to Merriam-Webster: to *cleave* means *to adhere firmly and closely; loyally and unwaveringly.* Whew! That'll preach all by itself. Firmly. Closely. Loyally. Unwaveringly. When you apply this to the institution of marriage, it sounds like a challenge waiting to happen. And truthfully, any deep relationship will test your loyalty—especially marriage.

So why would God create such a demanding design, knowing it would be hard to live out? Because He leads by example.

God is the epitome of covenant. Marriage is a reflection of His relationship with us. The Hebrew word *hesed (*pronounced heh-sed) describes God's covenantal, compassionate, and steadfast love for us. In *Ephesians 5:23–27,* we see that Jesus, our divine covering, loved His bride—the Church—so much that He gave Himself for her, sanctifying her with His sacrifice. He calls men to love their wives in the same way and calls wives to submit to their husbands, not as a burden, but as a divine alignment under a spiritual covering.

Now, ladies—before you roll your eyes and close the book, this isn't a detour into a submission lecture. It's a spiritual parallel meant to show how deeply valuable marriage is to God. And because marriage matters to God, you better believe it's on Satan's radar too.

The enemy hates covenant.

Whether your marriage is equally yoked or unequally yoked, the truth remains: Satan despises the union of one man and one woman. Because marriage, at its core, is ministry. He's been attacking it since the beginning. In the Garden of Eden, the command not to eat the forbidden fruit was given to Adam. But who did Satan approach? Eve. He bypassed the man to deceive the woman—not just to trick her, but to destroy the covenant they shared. And when Eve ate and Adam followed, their eyes were opened, their innocence was lost, and shame rushed in. Where there had been unity, there was now division. And what did Adam say? *"The woman that YOU gave me, gave me of the tree, and I ate."* (Genesis 3:12 KJV)

Geesh, Adam. A simple "Yes, I ate it," would've worked just fine! But that's what disobedience does—it brings dysfunction and division. And that same spirit is at work in marriages today.

So, what's the point of all this?

You—yes, *you* reading this—have an adversary. Whether you're a husband, wife, or even single, Satan doesn't like you. He wants your soul, and your spouse's soul, to spend eternity in hell with him. And I'm confident you don't want that—otherwise, you wouldn't be holding this book.

He wants to bait you into blame. He wants you to point the finger at your spouse and say, *"They made me do it. They made me cuss them out. They made me yell. They made me angry."*

But no, Adam. You ate that fruit.

You cursed them out.

You lost control.

You reacted.

Yes, maybe their actions triggered you, but you still have the power to choose your response. One of the fruits of the Spirit is self-control, and it is essential—especially when married to someone who doesn't share your faith. You don't have to curse. You don't have to yell. You don't have to eat the fruit of frustration.

You can choose to eat the fruit of self-discipline instead.

If we want to defeat the enemy in our marriages, we have to stop looking at our spouses as the problem and start inviting God to work on *us* first. It starts with a shift in us. That's the key. That's the freedom.

So hey, Eve. Hey, Adam—you don't have to eat the fruit.

Prayer

Lord, thank You for the divine covenant of marriage. Thank You for my spouse and all that they are—even when it's hard to see the good. Help me to remember that they are not my enemy; Satan is. Expose his tactics and give me the discernment to see clearly. Show me the areas in *me* that need healing, humility, and growth. God, forgive me for the times I didn't honor the sacredness of my marriage. Help me to walk worthy of this covenant. Let my actions reflect Your love, grace, and truth. Give me the self-control to reflect You, even in tension. Teach me to cleave—firmly, closely, loyally, and unwaveringly. In Jesus' name, Amen.

The Vow Within

Today, I vow to realign my view of marriage with God's original intent. Marriage is not just a legal agreement or emotional connection—it is a sacred covenant, divinely established and spiritually significant. It's a reflection of Christ and His Church, built on love, sacrifice, and commitment. I release the world's definitions and embrace God's design. I commit to honoring my covenant—not just with my words, but with my posture, my prayers, and my obedience to God's blueprint for oneness.

Reflections

How has my understanding of marriage been shaped by culture, pain, or unrealistic expectations? What does God's Word say about covenant—and how can I begin to walk in that truth today?

Two

Where Is Your Fruit?

"But the fruit of the Spirit is love, joy, peace, forbearance, kindness, goodness, faithfulness, gentleness, and self-control." — Galatians 5:22–23 KJV

For some of us, being unequally yoked to an unbeliever can be trying to our spirit man. I'm sure, if you're like me, when faced with tension and stress in marriage, it's easier to lash out in anger and frustration. Galatians 5:19–21 speaks of certain ungodly behaviors called the Works of the Flesh that are proof our connection to the Father has a kink in it. Things like idolatry, seditions, emulations—you might say, "Well, I don't struggle with those in my marriage," but what about hatred, strife, or wrath?

How do we fight against these fleshly desires? Thanks be to God that He didn't leave us hopeless or without a way to escape. To combat our carnality, He instructed us to demonstrate that His Spirit dwells within us by bearing fruit. "Fruit" in Greek is *karpòs*, meaning the result of something. When we received

Jesus as our Savior, we were sealed with His Spirit, assuring us that He would be with us by dwelling within us (Ephesians 1:13). The fruit—or proof—of the Spirit has nine parts, working simultaneously, growing bigger and stronger as we draw closer to God. But we can only continue to bear fruit if we stay connected to Christ.

In John 15, Jesus speaks of Himself as the vine, and we are His branches. Branches that don't have *karpòs*, or results, are cut off. But the branches that do bear fruit, He prunes—just like a gardener—so that they can continue to grow and prove that we are truly His disciples. Every time we face a challenge of the flesh, it's an opportunity to walk out the fruit of the Spirit. We cannot produce fruit on our own. It's only through the Holy Spirit—His strength in our weak moments—that we overcome. Every passed test is another chance to level up in our faith.

We don't have to live by the flesh or let it rule us. Romans 6 tells us that what we constantly offer ourselves to what will become our master, whether it's sin or righteousness. But when we accepted God into our hearts, He made us free from sin, giving us power over the flesh to now serve Him with righteousness and holiness.

So, in heated moments with your spouse, instead of letting wrath control you, replace that anger with peace. If you have hatred in your heart, replace it with love. Choose meekness instead of confrontation, remembering that your actions will speak louder than your words (1 Peter 3:1–2). Instead of being rebellious (which is witchcraft) against your spouse's needs, show kindness. We kill off the flesh by being fruitful in God. Deny yourself the things that you know are not pleasing to God in your marriage. Ask God to give you His strength when you feel weak.

The more we draw closer to God, the more of His fruit we will bear. The more we fall in love with Jesus, the more our fruit will grow.

Prayer

God, thank You so much for dwelling on the inside of me. Through Your Spirit, I am able to fight against the works of the flesh and walk in Your fruit. Holy Spirit, cultivate Your fruit in me. Let love, joy, peace, and the rest of the fruit flow through me and into my marriage. In Jesus name, Amen.

The Vow Within

Today, I vow to walk in the Spirit and not in my flesh. I will remain connected to the Vine so I may bear lasting fruit that transforms my home.

Reflections

What are some works of the flesh, written in or outside of Galatians 5, that you need to fight against in your marriage? What are some fruits of the Spirit that you need to intentionally implement?

Three

What Were You Thinking?

And be not conformed to this world: but be ye transformed by the renewing of your mind, that ye may prove what is that good, and acceptable, and perfect, will of God. — Romans 12:2 KJV

I know—you're tired. Tired of the arguments, the silence, the trying, the hoping. You've had enough! You've thought about walking away more than once, giving it all up. You're done.

But what if you're not? What if the breakthrough isn't in leaving—but in staying? What if God is revealing Himself in an unfamiliar way, asking you to remain just a little while longer because something deeper is being birthed?

In today's culture, walking away from marriage has become common. Countless marriages ending because it's not the "soft life" that we thought it would be. It's easy to quit when things don't go our way. People see those who fight for their marriages as foolish or naive. But staying and praying doesn't make you weak—it makes you wise. You can absolutely stay and fight for your marriage. Still, you can't fight without the right armor. And the most powerful weapon? A renewed mind.

I knew I needed a mind shift when I started waking up with negative thoughts about my husband. Before my feet hit the floor—before I even thanked God—I was already criticizing Kevin in my head. Although my home was quiet that morning, my thoughts were loud. Then I heard the Holy Spirit check me right in the kitchen: "You haven't even thanked Me today, but you've already torn your husband down in your thoughts." That conviction hit hard.

It didn't matter if he had done a hundred things right. One wrong thing? That's all I saw. And that's exactly what the enemy wants: to trap us in a cycle of criticism so we can no longer see the good, so that we can remain hopeless. Satan's earliest tactic in Scripture was to divide a husband and wife. He hasn't stopped since.

I used to roll my eyes at devotionals that said, "See your spouse through God's eyes." It felt unrealistic. But when I realized how the enemy uses our unrenewed thoughts as a weapon against our own homes, I knew something had to change.

As I write this, my husband still isn't a believer. And yet, God told me to write this devotional. I didn't want to—but obedience doesn't wait on comfort. If God can use my "yes" to help someone else, so be it. That "yes" begins with my mind—seeing Kevin not through my frustration but through God's heart.

Genesis 1:27 tells us that man and woman were created in God's image. In verse 31, God calls His creation very good. In fact, John

3:16 isn't just a scripture that we were taught to remember from our youth; it reveals the depth of God's love—He sent His Son to die a humiliating death for not only you, but also for your spouse. If He sees value in them, we must learn to see it too.

We must stop looking at our spouses with our natural eyes and allow the transformation of our mind to help us to see them through spiritual lenses. 2 Corinthians 10:5 urges us to cast down every false imagination. Those "always" and "never" thoughts must go. The persistent belief that they can never be saved must be broken. Philippians 4:8 teaches us to fix our minds on what is true, noble, pure, and praiseworthy. Is your spouse faithful? Kind? Hardworking? A good parent? Focus on that. If they didn't do all the dishes, thank them for the effort. Then talk—lovingly—about how they can improve.

What we meditate on becomes our mindset. And our mindset shapes how we speak and live. Complaints can turn into compliments when our thoughts are rooted in gratitude.

Prayer

Lord, renew my mind. Cleanse my thoughts and align them with Your truth. Silence the critical thoughts and fill me with Yours. Help me to cast down anything that exalts itself against the knowledge of who You are—and who my spouse is in You. Let me see them as You see them. And help me believe for what I cannot yet see. Help me to see my spouse the way You do—with compassion, patience, and honor. May my thoughts glorify You and reflect Your love. In Jesus' name, Amen.

The Vow Within

Today, I vow to take my thoughts captive—to cast down every imagination that doesn't align with God's truth about my marriage. I choose not to rehearse what's wrong, but to renew my mind with what is right. I will not allow assumptions, irritations, or past wounds to shape how I see my spouse. Instead, I will meditate on what is true, noble, just, pure, lovely, and praiseworthy. This mind of mine belongs to Christ—and with it, I choose to speak life.

Reflections

What toxic thoughts about my spouse do I need to cast down today? What truth from Romans 12:2, 2 Corinthians 10:5, or Philippians 4:8 will I cling to as a weapon against the enemy's lies?

____

____

____

____

____

____

____

Four

What Are You Looking At?

Looking unto Jesus the author and finisher of our faith; who for the joy that was set before him endured the cross, despising the shame, and is set down at the right hand of the throne of God. — Hebrews 12:2 KJV

Let's be real—comparison is a thief. And it doesn't just steal joy; it steals gratitude, peace, and perspective. One minute you're scrolling through your feed, and the next, you're questioning your marriage. That couple holding hands in the hallway. That coworker who gets surprise flowers. That friend who brags about how "amazing" their spouse is. And just like that, you start thinking, *Why can't my marriage be like that?*

Comparison feeds dissatisfaction. And dissatisfaction breeds resentment. It's not long before you stop seeing your spouse and only see their shortcomings—faults that are amplified in you when you idolize what you think looks right in someone else's life. What we see, hear, and digest can make us think contrary to what God says about our covenant. It then becomes our thoughts, our words, and eventually, our actions.

So, what are some practical ways to combat comparison in your marriage?

1. **Take a break from certain content.**
   Step back from content that makes you feel like your relationship is lacking. Your marriage is not theirs. Your journey is not theirs. The moment you begin measuring your covenant against someone else's highlight reel, you risk missing what God is doing right in your own backyard.

2. **Avoid lustful and distorted content.**
   Stay away from books, shows, or movies that portray intimacy in a distorted or ungodly way. If it leaves you feeling hopeless, envious, or lustful, remove it from your life immediately. Instead, consume content that edifies the sacred marriage you possess. Remember Hebrews 12:2: fix your eyes on Jesus—not your timeline, not your friends' relationships, not your expectations. Jesus is the author of your story. He knows the beginning, the middle, and the end. Go to Him for wisdom and strength, casting your discontentment on Him.

3. **Refuse to weaponize comparison at home.**
   Do not compare your spouse to your pastor, your church friends, or even to your old, more "spiritual" self. That

is a sure way to shut them down. No one wants to feel like they are constantly falling short. Comparison doesn't inspire change; it breeds shame.

4. **Stop using passive-aggressive tactics.**
   Don't leave a Bible open on their nightstand. Don't turn up the sermon volume when they walk in. Don't quote Scripture in place of sincere conversation. That is not intercession—it's manipulation.

5. **Show Jesus instead of shoving Him.**
   Let the fruit of the Spirit guide your actions. Show love. Show patience. Show kindness. Let your spouse see Jesus in how you handle even the hard moments. Edify them as the person they are now, seeing them the way God sees them.

6. **Embrace the balance of differences.**
   Don't just focus on the good or the bad. Recognize that each of you carries qualities, traits, and characteristics the other needs for your marriage to be fruitful and multiply

7. **Communicate your needs with love.**
   If you feel unfulfilled, speak up in love. Allow your spouse the opportunity to fill you up. Healthy communication builds connection and strengthens your covenant.

Remember, your spouse may not share your faith yet, but that doesn't mean God isn't working. Philippians 4:11 reminds us to be content in all things. 1 Timothy 6:6 teaches that godliness with contentment is great gain. And Hebrews 13:5 calls us to keep our hearts free from covetousness, knowing that God is always with us.

If your grass is looking brown, don't abandon the soil—start planting and watering. Plant seeds of honor, grace, patience, respect, humility, and love. Then water them with prayer and the Word.

This journey isn't about having a perfect marriage. It's about trusting a perfect God with an imperfect person—and choosing to see your spouse through the eyes of Christ, not filtered ones. Trust His process.

Prayer

Lord, I confess I've let comparison cloud how I see my marriage. Help me to stop looking sideways and start looking upward—to You. I've fantasized about someone else's story and overlooked the one You're writing for me. Help me be content and grateful for the covenant You've entrusted to me. Teach me to plant good seeds and water them with Your truth. Redirect my gaze from what's missing to what You're making. In Jesus' name, Amen.

The Vow Within

Today, I vow to stop measuring my marriage against the highlight reels of others. I choose to guard my heart against comparison and fix my eyes on Christ, the true Author of this covenant.

I commit to watering my own grass—with patience, love, and prayer—trusting that God is doing a work in me and in my spouse that is sacred, unseen, and still unfolding.

Reflections

Where have I allowed comparison to cloud my contentment in marriage? What are three things I can begin to thank God for today in my spouse—and how will I intentionally water those areas this week?

Five

Help My Unbelief

"And all things, whatsoever ye shall ask in prayer, believing, ye shall receive." — Matthew 21:22 KJV

As I mentioned before, this devotional isn't about focusing solely on the change we want to see in our spouses—it's about the change that needs to happen within us. And here's the truth: we can't expect transformation if we don't first believe it's possible.

It's easy to have faith when things are going well. Maybe they came to church and participated in worship. Maybe they finally agreed to that marriage conference you've been begging them to attend—and they even gave feedback. In moments like that, believing feels natural.

But what about the hard days? When they're cursing at you? When they're doing things you know are completely against what you believe? Can you still hold on to hope in those moments, or do you throw up your hands and walk away?

The title of today's devotional comes from Mark 9:24. A man brings his son to Jesus, desperate for deliverance from a spirit that's been tormenting him since childhood. This demon had tried to kill the boy—throwing him into fire and water. Jesus tells the father, *"If you can believe, all things are possible."* And the father cries out, *"Lord, I believe—help my unbelief!"*

At first glance, it might sound like a contradiction. But I believe he was covering all bases. He was saying, *"Lord, I do believe. But if there's any part of me that doubts—help that part, too."* He needed the miracle, and there was no room for hesitation.

Friend, the same way that spirit tried to destroy that boy is the same way the enemy is trying to destroy your marriage. Are you desperate enough to believe for deliverance? Can you cry out, *"Jesus, help my unbelief when it comes to my marriage"*?

In my own marriage, choosing to believe is a daily decision. Living with someone who doesn't share your faith is not easy. I constantly have to renew my mind, change my tone, apologize, rinse, and repeat. But I choose not to doubt—because my husband's soul depends on it.

If I pray for him and get up filled with doubt, I've already forfeited the battle; I'm immediately defeated. Either I believe God or I don't. And yes, that sounds simple—but living it out is another story.

That's why I have to be renewed in the Word every single day. When I fall short, I repent and get back up. And little by little, God keeps building my faith. Sometimes through the peace He gives me in the storm. Other times, it's through giving me the spirit of "shut up," so I can hear my husband's heart.

Little by little, God keeps showing me glimpses of what could be—if I don't faint.

Matthew 21:21 tells us that if we believe and do not doubt, mountains will move. James 1:6–8 reminds us that when we doubt, we're like a wave tossed by the sea. That kind of instability blocks our prayers from bearing fruit.

That convicted me! Could my doubt be what's delaying the breakthrough I've been praying for? Am I praying on my knees just to get back up in doubt?

It's time to stop doubting and start believing again. Stop throwing in the towel every time your spouse acts out. They don't think like you. They're not convicted like you. And they may not even care about what you care about—but that's exactly why God called *you* to stand in the gap.

You have to believe for them when they can't believe for themselves.

So, let me ask you plainly: are you a believer...or a doubter?

Prayer

God, there are times when I can see the light at the end of the tunnel—and then it fades with every disappointment. I want to keep believing that my spouse will come to know You as their Lord and Savior, just as I have. Your Word says it is not Your will for any to perish, but for all to come to repentance. I pray that my spouse is in that number. Help my unbelief when my hope starts to dwindle.

Let Your Word restore the joy of salvation and let my actions reflect that joy. In Jesus' name, Amen.

The Vow Within

Today, I vow to believe again. I will choose faith over fear, intercession over irritation, and trust over doubt. I declare that my prayers are not in vain—and neither is my love. I believe God is still writing our story. And I believe He's not finished yet.

Reflections

Where in my marriage have I allowed doubt to take root? What promise from God do I need to revisit, believe again, and declare over my spouse with bold faith? Write a prayer of faith—even if it starts with, *"Lord, help my unbelief."*

____

____

____

____

____

____

____

____

____

____

Six

We Are Family

"What therefore God hath joined together, let not man put asunder." — Mark 10:9 KJV

As we saw in Day 1, marriage is a covenant—a sacred union between you, your spouse, and God. Whether or not your union includes children, family is one of God's most powerful vessels for transformation within our homes and others. That's why Satan's first attack on earth was aimed at the family.

When Adam and Eve disobeyed God, their unity was fractured. Sin entered. Division followed. And the consequences reached the next generation. In Genesis 4, their sons Cain and Abel brought offerings to God—one accepted, one rejected. *Jealousy turned into rage, Cain killed his brother, and he was cast out.* Adam and Eve didn't just lose one child—they lost two.

This is what happens when we let the enemy divide our homes. One fracture can lead to generational loss. I've heard countless stories of adults who were once hurting children—acting out because they lacked the love, covering, or guidance of a united home. Some are still grieving that absence decades later.

When a family breaks, the ripple effect is real.

Maybe your family is facing that kind of fracture now. A child in rebellion. Ongoing financial stress. Constant tension in your marriage. Maybe you've spoken the word "divorce" aloud—or you're still grieving someone who once held the family together. Whatever the struggle, it's not too big for God. But He can only heal what we surrender to Him.

God doesn't allow conflict to destroy us. He allows it to develop us. Disagreements can become divine moments—if we let them. They are opportunities to hear each other's thoughts, opinions, and hearts. But it takes humility, wisdom, and the presence of the Holy Spirit to help steward us in doing and saying those things that will bring peace within conflict.

Scripture gives us tools for this:

- Practice the fruit of the Spirit (Galatians 5:22–23).
- Be quick to listen and slow to speak (James 1:19–20).
- Don't jump to conclusions (Proverbs 18:13).
- Speak life and protection over your children (Ps. 112:2; 127:3-5).
- Declare Scripture over your finances (Ps. 112:3; Prov 10:22).
- Pray for wisdom and peace (1 Kg. 3:9; Ps. 4:8. 29:11).

These faithful acts have the power to reshape not only your marriage—but your legacy.

1 Corinthians 7:10–16 speaks directly to the believer married to an unbeliever. Paul urges us not to walk away simply because of spiritual differences. Your spouse—and your children—are sanctified through your walk with Christ. Even if they don't believe yet, your faith is covering them.

Verse 16 asks, *"How do you know, wife, whether you will save your husband?"* The truth? You don't. But God does. And He honors obedience.

Now hear this: we are not called to remain in marriages marked by abuse, infidelity, or abandonment. But outside of those situations, we must not confuse discomfort with release. Sometimes the suffering we endure is refining us. Producing perseverance, character, and hope (Romans 5:3–5). 1 Peter 4:13 even tells us to rejoice in suffering with Christ—because when we do, He meets us with comfort and strength.

The Biblical principles that you implement within your union will change the trajectory of your family and impact your bloodline. You're not just holding your marriage together. You're holding up a legacy. And God is holding you.

Prayer

Lord, there are moments when I grow weary of the conflict that constantly arises in my home. It feels like we argue more than we agree. But I know that You are able to bring peace, unity, and understanding. Help me see where I need to grow—where I need to listen better, love better, and lead better. Give me direction, discipline, and discernment. Strengthen me to fight for my family—not just for today, but for generations to come. In Jesus' name, Amen.

The Vow Within

Today, I vow to see my family as God sees it—chosen, covered, and worth fighting for. I commit to stewarding this marriage and this legacy with grace, humility, and faith. Even when it's hard. Even when I feel alone. I believe God is building something eternal through my obedience.

Reflections

What is God showing me about my family today? Where is He asking me to step in, intercede, or surrender? What part of my family's legacy is He calling me to rebuild through prayer and faithfulness?

____

____

____

____

____

____

Seven

70 x 7

"Then Peter came to Him and said, 'Lord, how often shall my brother sin against me, and I forgive him? Up to seven times?' Jesus said to him, 'I do not say to you seven times, but seventy times seven.'" — Matthew 18:21-22 KJV

Jesus wasn't suggesting a literal 490-time forgiveness limit. He was making it clear: forgiveness is ongoing, boundless, and not something we keep score on. And while forgiveness is hard in any relationship, it can feel especially difficult in marriage.

Maybe your spouse said something hurtful. Or perhaps the wound runs deeper—like betrayal or infidelity. Whatever it is, forgiveness may feel impossible. But it isn't.

When we forgive, we mirror the heart of God, the one who offered us forgiveness that we could never earn. Colossians 3:13 says we must forgive as we have been forgiven. If our perfect and holy God forgives us repeatedly, who are we to withhold forgiveness from our spouse? Forgiveness isn't optional. It's commanded.

In Matthew 6:12, Jesus teaches us to pray, asking the Father to "forgive us our debts, as we also have forgiven our debtors." He adds in verses 14-15 that if we forgive others, God will forgive us—but if we don't, neither will He forgive us. That's a sobering truth. When we walk in unforgiveness, we walk in rebellion. We become idolaters, elevating our own will over God's (Ephesians 2:2).

Unforgiveness is not a weapon to punish the one who hurt you. It isn't your job to hold onto anger or bitterness. Ephesians 4:31-32 calls us to let go of all malice and instead walk in kindness and compassion. And Romans 12:19 reminds us that vengeance belongs to the Lord. Instead of praying, "God, get them!" we must pray, "God, open their eyes. Soften their heart."

Even if your spouse never apologizes, you still have a mandate to forgive. Forgiveness isn't weakness. It's spiritual maturity. It's freedom. It's peace. When you forgive, you break the chains of bitterness that Satan tries to use to hold you captive. You become a living testimony of God's grace in your own home.

I struggled deeply with this. I believed that intimacy—whether emotional or physical—should result in behavioral change. When it didn't, I became angry. That anger led to resentment. My tone shifted. My heart hardened. I stopped serving. I became mean.

Yes, there should be conversations around what hurt you. But don't let bitterness speak for you. Let God lead those conversations. Let Him prepare your heart before you confront your spouse. True forgiveness allows room for healing and growth.

Willingly forgive, letting the blemish of the offense go, inviting the new scent of forgiveness to penetrate your home. Let forgiveness become routine, forgiving frequently and freely.

Through forgiveness, we soften our hearts to hear God's voice again. We realign with His will. We allow Him to guide us toward unity and peace in our marriages. We set our hearts free. We set our marriages free.

Prayer

God, thank You for forgiving me over and over again. Teach me to extend that same grace to my spouse. Help me forgive when it's hard, when it hurts, and even when I don't receive an apology. I want to honor You with my obedience and walk in the freedom that forgiveness brings. In Jesus' name, Amen.

The Vow Within

I vow to forgive as Christ forgave me. I choose to release the weight of bitterness and invite God to bring healing. I will not hold past offenses over my spouse's head. I will walk in grace, love, and obedience.

Reflections

What offenses am I still holding onto in my heart? What would it look like to truly forgive my spouse and move forward in freedom?

Eight
It's About God, Not Your Spouse

"Wives, be submissive to your own husbands, that even if some do not obey the Word, they, without a word, may be won by the conduct of their wives. Likewise, husbands, live with your wives in an understanding way, showing honor to her as the weaker vessel, since they are heirs with you of the grace of life, so that your prayers may not be hindered." — 1 Peter 3:1,7 KJV

In the beginning, Kevin and I were in what felt like marital bliss. He worked overnight, and I would stay up for hours talking with him until it was time for bed or until he came home. We couldn't get enough of each other.

Then something changed. He began slipping back into his old ways—ways that didn't include Christ. I was confused, heartbroken, and even more so when he confessed that he had only pretended to be saved—for me. What I thought was an equally yoked marriage...wasn't.

I found myself constantly arguing and fussing over things that seemed clearly right or wrong to me. But he didn't see it that way. My godly conduct—before his confession—was now being tested in the tension of our unequally yoked marriage. And I'll be honest—it's taken nearly twelve years for me to begin understanding what these verses in 1 Peter truly mean.

I didn't realize it then, but my attitude was misrepresenting Christ—the very image Kevin was supposed to see through me. I was the only example of Jesus he knew, and I was doing a poor job.

I'll never forget leaving church one day and watching him immediately turn up secular music in the car. When I complained, he said, "Church is over." My frustration grew. I yelled. I argued. I tried to correct him—right after we'd just heard a Word that clearly hadn't taken root in me either. He called me out. And that cut deep.

But it made me reflect. God used those moments to show me that godliness isn't proven by how you dress or how kind you are when things are good. It's proven by how you respond in difficulty, disagreement, and mockery. It's your posture when you're misunderstood. It's how you speak to your spouse in conflict. How you show love even when you don't get love in return.

That's what truly reflects Christ.

God had to show me that being godly means being submitted—to Him first. It means embodying the fruit of the Spirit: being quick to forgive, slow to speak, slow to anger, quick to listen. Even when your spouse isn't leading well. Even when you feel like giving up. These are the things that can win over an unbelieving spouse—not by words, but by conduct.

When we shift our focus off our spouse and back onto God, it gets easier to carry His heart. God honors that kind of surrender. He sees that your focus is on Him and not just the shortcomings of your marriage.

But when we fixate on what our spouse isn't, we miss who God *is*. We become obsessed with changing them instead of being changed ourselves. We start believing that our works can save them, when in truth, only God can.

I once heard a woman testify about her backslidden husband returning to Christ. It wasn't because she pressured him. It was because he saw her genuine relationship with God—and it stirred something in him. That testimony rocked me!

I realized I'd spent so much time focused on Kevin's flaws, I forgot to see what was right about him. I idolized the problem. I worshipped the idea of a restored marriage more than the One who restored me.

Yes, I prayed. Yes, I worshipped. But so much of it was wrapped up in marriage restoration: God, I worship You because I know You can change him. Fix us. Save him." When was the last time I simply said, "God, thank You for who You are—before I was ever a wife."

I was consumed. Every moment of the day was filled with thoughts about what Kevin wasn't doing. I wasn't leaving space for God to move in his heart because I was trying to move it for Him.

Please hear me: pray for your spouse. Intercede for your marriage. But don't idolize it.

Get in God's Word and let it change *you*. Let it shape your heart, your thoughts, your tone. Let it make you Christ-centered, not spouse-centered. Because when you do, your spouse will notice. The transformation in *you* might just stir transformation in *them*.

Don't draw near to God for your spouse's sake. Draw near to God because He's worthy. Be less spouse-centered and more Christ-centered.

Prayer

Father, You created this world. You are God over all things—my marriage included. You have all power and control. Help me to relinquish mine. I release the burden of trying to fix what only You can heal. Help me to fix my eyes on You. Refocus my heart on You. Shift my focus from frustration to faith. As I grow closer to You, shape me into someone who reflects Your heart—so that even in my silence, my life speaks. In Jesus' name, Amen.

The Vow Within

Today, I recommit to honoring God first. I vow to reflect Christ in how I live, not just in what I say. I will no longer carry the burden of transformation—I surrender that to the One who transforms hearts. I vow to shift my gaze from the flaws of my spouse to the faithfulness of my God. I choose to serve God first and trust Him with the heart of my marriage.

Reflections

Where have I been trying to do God's job in my marriage? What areas of control do I need to release to Him today? How can my life reflect Christ more consistently to my spouse? In what areas have I made my spouse or marriage an idol? What would it look like to re-center my focus on God today?

____

____

____

____

____

____

____

____

____

____

____

____

____

____

____

____

Nine

Stop Rehearsing Bad Moments

""Do not remember the former things, Nor consider the things of old." — Isaiah 43:18 KJV

While it's important to remember the amazing things God has done for us—the testimonies that have helped us overcome—some things we simply need to let go.

In Genesis 19, Lot and his family were instructed to flee Sodom and Gomorrah because God was about to destroy it. They were told not to look back. But Lot's wife did. What was so bad about her looking back? First, she disobeyed a direct command from God. Second, theologians believe she looked back because she still desired the very place God had just delivered her from. Whatever her reason, her disobedience caused her to be turned into a pillar of salt.

That may sound extreme, but let's look at what really happened: Lot's wife was instantly frozen in place—unable to move forward—because she was too focused on what was behind her. She couldn't walk into the future God had prepared for her and her family because she was too stuck in the past.

I don't know about you, but I can relate to her more than I'd like to admit. As I mentioned before, I used to rehearse every offense Kevin had done to me. It became my daily routine. I'd replay moments that annoyed me, things I didn't understand and labeled as dumb, and situations where I knew I was right, and he was wrong. Those memories fueled my anger and pride, making me feel justified in my emotions toward him.

But the more I clung to those moments, the more bound I felt. And the more bound I felt, the further I drifted from God. As I distanced myself from Him, I found my marriage following the same pattern. Instead of casting my cares on the Lord, I held onto them tightly—along with bitterness and resentment. My heart hardened toward Kevin, and it kept me from praying for him.

I was doing exactly what the enemy wanted: giving up my faith that Jesus could do the impossible. Giving up hope that Kevin would ever give his life to Christ. And that would've been catastrophic—not just for my marriage, but for my family's future and Kevin's soul.

So, I made a choice: I stopped looking back. I began casting my cares on Jesus. And now, when old memories try to resurface, I remind myself—I've already forgiven him. I can forgive him again. I can address the issue without anger or bitterness because my heart has changed.

We can't change the past. We can only change the present.

So, what are you still looking back at? What unresolved offense are you silently holding onto? Because if you've truly forgiven your spouse, you wouldn't be dragging yesterday into today.

I'm not saying you shouldn't hold your spouse accountable. But if you're still bringing up something from a month ago—something you claimed to have forgiven—you haven't truly let it go. And if you continue to shame your spouse for resolved offenses, how can they ever feel free?

Neither of you can move forward if the past keeps playing on repeat.

Instead, be thankful for today. Rejoice in it. Choose to see the good in this moment and steward it well. Because while we can't change the past, we can absolutely change the outcome of our future—by how we choose to show up today.

Prayer

God, my past is holding me hostage. I keep rehearsing offenses because I don't see progress in my spouse. Help me shift my focus. Help me love them where they are and trust You with the rest. Teach me to stop looking back and walk forward in the freedom You've given me. In Jesus' name, Amen.

The Vow Within

I vow to stop rehearsing old wounds. I choose to release the past and open my heart to the present. I will forgive, not just with my words, but with my actions—and trust God to do the healing that I cannot.

Reflections

What memories or past offenses do I need to surrender today? How will choosing to release them create space for peace and progress in my marriage?

Ten

Love the One You're With

"Love suffers long and is kind; love does not envy; love does not parade itself, is not [a]puffed up;"— 1 Corinthians 13:4 NKJV

There's a joke I laugh at every time: In marriage, there are three rings—the engagement ring, the wedding ring, and the suffer-ring!

But seriously, marriage will bring some level of suffering, especially for those of us whose spouses don't share our faith. Conflict becomes almost inevitable—disagreements over how to raise the kids, what's morally acceptable, or even whether Halloween is harmless or harmful. You've prayed. You've cried. And still, it feels like your marriage is stuck.

But suffering doesn't mean you're out of God's will. In fact, sometimes it proves you're right in the center of it.

Hebrews 12:11 reminds us that although discipline isn't pleasant, it produces a harvest of righteousness for those who are trained by it. And sometimes, that discipline comes through delayed prayers. God hears you. He sees the tears. But He's also growing something in you—patience, maturity, and endurance. James 1:3–4 tells us that suffering produces patience, and patience makes us whole.

So how do we love our spouses through the suffering?

First, we take our eyes off the pain and put them on Jesus—the ultimate Sufferer. When we obsess over our problems, we lose sight of the glory that God can bring through them. We begin giving more power to the struggle than to the Savior. And yes, it's hard—especially when the same disagreement keeps showing up like clockwork. When your spouse seems to be getting worse. When their salvation feels further away than ever.

But worry can't change hearts. Instead, focus on the One who can. The more we focus on Him, the more we become like Him and the more clearly we see through His eyes. Our focus shifts from the pain to the purpose. From suffering to surrender. And when God sees that we trust Him, He moves according to our faith.

1 Corinthians 13 is often called the "Love Chapter." Out of everything Paul could have said first, he started with this: *Love suffers long*. What a hard pill to swallow! Then right after that? *Love is kind.* So, in my suffering... I still have to be kind? Whew! If that doesn't feel like God's sense of humor, I don't know what does.

But God is always honest with us. He doesn't sugarcoat the hard parts. He tells us straight up—this journey of love is going to stretch us. And who better to lead us than the One who daily suffers our ignorance, rejection, and disobedience with grace?

How many of us feel ignored or rejected in marriage? And yet, God calls us to be kind in return. To love like He does. To mirror the grace He's shown us. To be more like Him, especially through the suffering.

Prayer

God, allowing Your Son to die on the cross for our sins was the ultimate example of love. If Jesus could die for me, I can die to my flesh and love my spouse the way You've commanded me to. I am able, because You are able. In Jesus' name, Amen.

The Vow Within

I vow to suffer well and love well. I commit to showing kindness even in discomfort, trusting that God is shaping me into the image of Christ.

Reflections

Read 1 Corinthians 13 again—even if you've read it your whole life. Let it read *you*. What is 1 Corinthians 13 revealing about how I love? What verses convict you? How can I love my spouse better this week—through patience and kindness? Where do you need to grow? Ask the Holy Spirit to transform your heart, and you'll begin to see your spouse through Christ's eyes.

Eleven

Turn Away from Pride

"Pride goeth before destruction, and an haughty spirit before a fall."— Proverbs 16:18 KJV

There is a healthy side of pride- being proud of your loved one's accomplishments. Taking pride in your work. But scripture warns us about how self-centered pride can be disastrous. It's even considered one of the seven daily sins.

It can cause catastrophic damage to our relationships when we want to be heard and proven right. It causes us to feel justified in our wrongs and blinded to our own faults and failures and ultimately leads us to rebellion.

Too often, I felt justified in mistreating my husband because of how he treated me. I believed that if people knew what I was going through, they'd side with me—and they did. Their support only fueled my pride. But just like Proverbs 16:18 warns, I fell. I stepped out of God's will and out of my marriage, still feeling justified in the eyes of others. I was so blinded, I couldn't see how foolish I looked.

That's what pride does. It puffs you up and hardens your heart. It keeps you from seeing how your behavior affects others. It convinces you that your way is right, even when it clearly isn't. Scripture is clear—God detests pride. It was pride that got Lucifer kicked out of Heaven (Ezekiel 28:17). And it's pride that keeps so many of us stuck in cycles of pain and rebellion.

The Word warns us over and over about the danger of pride:

- **Psalm 10:4** — The proud don't seek God; He's not even in their thoughts.

- **2 Timothy 3:2–5** — In the last days, people will be lovers of themselves, boastful, proud. Paul says to stay away from them.

- **Psalm 59:12** — Pride traps us in lies and curses.

- **Psalm 73:6** — Pride wraps around us like chains.

- **Proverbs 11:2** — Pride brings shame. Wisdom follows humility.

- **Proverbs 14:3** — Foolish speech is rooted in pride.

And I could go on. Scripture doesn't just suggest that pride is harmful—it screams it!

When I realized that my justified, prideful behavior was leading me away from God, I had to repent. I had to surrender my false sense of control—because that's what pride really is. A lie that says *I* can fix things. That *I* can change hearts. But only God can do that. The heart of the king is in His hand (Proverbs 21:1), not mine.

My actions, no matter how "deserved," are never justified if they dishonor Christ. God didn't call me to be a judge in my marriage. He called me to be a witness. A vessel of grace. And once I surrendered my pride, He began the work of softening both our hearts.

Pride ruins marriages. Pride resists God. And pride keeps us from seeing ourselves, our relationships and God, clearly.

Prayer

Pride is killing my marriage, God. I see it now. My high-mindedness is keeping me in a cycle of arrogance, and it's bleeding through my character. I can feel the drift from You, and it scares me. Please change my heart. Help me surrender my pride so I can reflect You more clearly to my spouse. In Jesus' name, Amen.

The Vow Within

I vow to lay down my pride. I will not let self-righteousness rob me of God's presence or His promises in my marriage. I choose humility over justification.

Reflections

What is God revealing to me about pride in my heart? In what ways has pride shaped my responses toward my spouse, and how can I begin to surrender it today?

Twelve

What Did You Say?

"Death and life are in the power of the tongue: and they that love it shall eat the fruit thereof." — Proverbs 18:21 KJV

We have the power to change the dynamic of our marriage through what we say. If our words are edifying, our spouses feel encouraged. If our words are harsh, they feel defeated. We can either speak life into our marriage—or slowly kill it—with our tongues. Those who speak life are eating the fruit of the Spirit and drawing closer to God, despite what they see. But those who speak death are feeding the flesh and drifting away from Him. Either way, our words have weight.

I know it's hard to always say the kind thing in frustrating moments. Trust me, I still struggle with letting things get under my skin. In those moments, I want to lash out and say the first hurtful thing that comes to mind. But that's just it—what comes out of our mouths is proof of what's inside us. If we harbor bitterness, it will eventually spill out.

If we believe our spouses are lazy or lacking, that belief will flow from our hearts to our mouths, tearing them down. Luke 6 says that both the good and bad in a person's heart will eventually be spoken. So, when I notice what I'm saying—and how I'm saying it—I must check what I'm storing inside. Satan is listening, and he'll use every careless word to torment and accuse. I know because Kevin told me. He shared how my words made him feel small, discouraged, and ashamed. And that hit me hard. If you can doubt yourself long enough, you can start doubting God.

On the other hand, kind words bring life. In Genesis 50, after everything his brothers had done to him, Joseph spoke kindly to them and comforted them. His words disarmed them. That's powerful. And it's biblical. Ephesians 4:29 tells us to speak only what is good and useful for building others up. When I do that—when I make a conscious effort to build Kevin up—I see the difference. His posture shifts. His smile returns. He feels seen and valued. That's the power of words.

Too many marriages die because we refuse to look past our hurts and spew venom instead. I've heard stories of good men walking away—not because they didn't love their wives, but because they were constantly torn down. The same goes for women. It's not always about what you say; it's how you say it. Proverbs 15:1 says that a gentle answer turns away wrath, but harsh words stir up anger.

Your tone matters. Your timing matters. Even when your words are true, they can still wound if said without love. So, speak life. Speak Scripture. Declare what God says over your marriage:

- *My marriage will not end in divorce.*
- *My unsaved spouse will be saved and filled with the Holy Spirit.*
- *My family will serve the Lord.*
- *We are covered and protected by God.*

Choose today to stop killing your marriage with careless words. Let hurtful communication go. Speak what builds. Speak what heals. Speak freedom. Speak life.

Prayer

The words I've spoken over my marriage have wounded more than they've healed. Lord, I want to speak life, but I can't do it without You. Convict me when I'm tempted to lash out. Teach me to speak with love and wisdom. Fill my mouth with words that restore, not destroy. In Jesus' name, Amen.

The Vow Within

I vow to guard my tongue and speak life. I will not allow my emotions to dictate my language. I will build, not break.

Reflections

What are some damaging words I've spoken that I need to repent for? What life-giving declarations can I begin speaking over my spouse and marriage today?

Thirteen
Give Grace

"And of his fulness have all we received, and grace for grace." —John 1:16 KJV

Grace is best given when the one receiving it doesn't expect it. It's unmerited. But sometimes we hold it hostage as if it belongs to us. We give grace because it has been freely given to us. Jesus' dying was Him showing grace to an undeserving people. As His followers, we are called to reflect that same character.

Marriage is the most intimate relationship you can have. You share experiences and vulnerabilities you wouldn't with anyone else. But with that vulnerability can come deep hurt. The ones closest to us often hurt us the worst. Words spoken in harsh tones, aggressive actions, and wounded feelings can cause damage. And while some of those actions may seem intentional, many aren't. In those tense moments, are you quick to condemn, or quick to give grace? Are you able to look past the tone and the tension to see their pain and point of view?

In heated moments, it's easy to feel unloved or discarded. But are those feelings rooted in truth? Does your spouse truly not love you, or are they just expressing themselves poorly? Is your perception based on past actions? Why is it so hard to extend grace?

Marriage should never be performance-based. We don't give grace only when our spouses satisfy us. Love is grace. If we are not walking in love, we can't walk in grace. Pride depletes a marriage. If your spouse keeps missing the mark, maybe it's time to change the way you communicate. Perhaps your message isn't coming across clearly. Repeating yourself doesn't always work. Instead, try to see through their lens. Ask them how you can better express your heart. Proverbs 3:34 says God gives grace to the humble. So, in humility, we receive grace, and in humility, we give it.

Don't hold their sin over their head. Forgive quickly. Don't let offenses simmer and spoil the soil of your heart. If you can't agree in the moment, save the conversation for a calm one. And once you forgive, give them space and time to prove that they heard your heart. Let God do the work in them.

Seek to serve rather than be served. When we serve our spouses in unlikely circumstances, we serve the Lord. John 12:26 reminds us that God honors those who serve. But serve with intentionality and consistency. Don't let emotions dictate when you serve and when you withhold. Pray for peace when anger rises. Ask God to move in your heart. When your spouse sees you serve them when they least deserve it, their heart will begin to soften—to you and to God. Through grace, through love, you are helping reconcile them back to God.

Prayer

God, thank You for the undeserved grace You've shown me throughout my life. Help me to show my spouse grace through the humility I find in You. Soften their heart toward You as I continue to serve them in Your strength. In Jesus' name, Amen.

The Vow Within

I vow to extend grace, not because it is deserved, but because it reflects the heart of Christ within me.

Reflections

In what specific areas can I show my spouse more grace, and how can I begin practicing that today?

____

____

____

____

____

____

____

____

____

____

Fourteen
Be Faithful Anyway

"Fear none of those things which thou shalt suffer: behold, the devil shall cast some of you into prison, that ye may be tried; and ye shall have tribulation ten days: be thou faithful unto death, and I will give thee a crown of life." — Revelation 2:10 KJV

One of the hardest things to do when faced with division in a marriage is to remain faithful. Whether spiritual or physical, God expects us to remain faithful because it is a foundational quality for any marriage. Our spouses are blessed by it, and so are our children, grandchildren, friends, and even our communities.

To be transparent, in my own marriage, I've been unfaithful both spiritually and physically. In fact, my spiritual unfaithfulness led to my physical unfaithfulness. Our marriage took a turn for the worse, and I felt uncovered. But instead of running to God, I got distracted. Even after reconciling with my husband, I felt unheard. I became numb and let my guard down. I fell for the enemy's trap because I had taken my eyes off God. I stopped reading my Word and serving my husband. I ignored warning signs and believed I wouldn't fall. I thought the grass was greener. And just like most people find out—it was not.

My unfaithfulness to God opened a door to experiences that still haunt me. Isaiah 26:3 says God will keep us in perfect peace if our minds are stayed on Him. But my focus had shifted. I didn't trust that He would answer my prayers. I couldn't see His faithfulness because my unfaithfulness had blinded me. Scriptures like 2 Thessalonians 3:3 no longer resonated: *"But the Lord is faithful, who will establish you and keep you from evil."*

When we allow our hearts to harden toward our spouses, unbelief creeps in. We start doubting the very promises God gave us about our marriages. Numbers 23:19 reminds us that God does not lie—so why do we doubt? Because we allow what we see to alter what we believe. But our outcomes are determined by our obedience and faithfulness. Choosing facts over faith kills hope. When your faith wavers, ask God for strength. 2 Timothy 2:13 tells us that even when we are faithless, He remains faithful.

What are the benefits of loyalty? Proverbs 3:3–4 says that when we walk in faithfulness and consistency, we find favor and good success in the sight of God and man. You may feel like your efforts—your prayers, fasting, your self-control—are going unnoticed. But God sees them. And your spouse sees them too. God will reward you, both now and in eternity.

So, how do we grow in faithfulness? Be trustworthy, like Daniel. When others tried to trap him, they couldn't find fault in him because of his faithfulness. Even in the lion's den, Daniel trusted God—and God protected him.

Be obedient to God. Deuteronomy 28:9 promises that if we obey and walk in His ways, He will establish us. We are faithful to our spouses because Christ is faithful to us. Our loyalty says, "God, I trust You, no matter what."

Prayer

God, You said a faithful man will abound in blessings. Help me remain faithful to You so my family may be blessed. Strengthen me when I'm weary and help me stand when my loyalty is tested. In Jesus' name, Amen.

The Vow Within

I vow to remain faithful in word, thought, and deed—not because it's easy, but because it's holy.

Reflections

In what areas does your faithfulness need strengthening, and how can you invite God into those areas today?

____

____

____

____

Fifteen
Praying Over Traumas

"The righteous cry, and the Lord heareth, and delivereth them out of all their troubles." — Psalm 34:17 KJV

When two people come together, they most likely bring their past hurts, pains, and traumas into the relationship. Being unequally yoked can heighten those experiences. You'd be surprised how a disagreement about dishes can turn into an argument rooted in past emotional wounds. Relationships often expose the burdens we carry or the ones we've buried deep inside.

Trauma can stem from various sources: the death of a loved one, physical abuse in childhood, or hurtful words spoken that became lies you now believe. These experiences shape how we respond to conflict. A sharp tone, a certain word, or specific action can trigger memories of when we felt unsafe or unloved. And these reactions can create fresh trauma within our marriage.

Maybe you grew up in a household filled with yelling and chaos, and now, during disagreements, your tone escalates without thinking. Perhaps you learned to withdraw because you never felt heard. These are learned responses—trauma responses—and while they may have helped you survive back then, they're hurting your marriage now. You've considered therapy but fear reliving old wounds.

Whatever your past looks like, it's not too big for God. 1 Peter 5:7 reminds us to cast our cares on Him because He cares for us. He doesn't just want to hear about your pain—He wants to heal it. What happened to you does not define you or disqualify your purpose.

Let your healing help your spouse heal too. If they've shared their traumas with you, protect that vulnerability. Pray for them—out loud, if they're willing, and in private, if not. Fast for their healing. Intercede the way you would want someone to pray for you.

Maybe the trauma happened inside the marriage. Words were said. Actions were taken. Trust was broken. You both carry wounds now. But healing begins when someone chooses humility and takes the first step. Repent for your part. Forgive their part. And seek help together.

Consider counseling. Make a plan for what healing looks like in your home. True restoration requires intentional steps. Here are some keys to healing:

- Identify your wounds so they don't create further damage.

- Ask God to reveal the root of your trauma.

- Don't weaponize your spouse's trauma. Protect it.
- Ask God for strength to overcome wounds and traumas.

Prayer

God, thank You for the ability to pray for my marriage. We have both experienced traumas before and during our marriage. Today, I cast all our hurt onto You because You are strong enough to carry it. Heal our hearts. Renew our minds. Draw us closer to one another as we draw closer to You. Amen.

The Vow Within

I vow to recognize the pain within myself and my spouse, and to seek healing—together, in Christ.

Reflections

What traumatic experiences do I need to surrender to God for healing? What's keeping me from forgiving myself or my spouse?

____

____

____

____

____

Sixteen

Breaking Generational Curses

"Christ has redeemed us from the curse of the law, being made a curse for us." — Galatians 3:13 KJV

Now that we've identified the traumas and wounds we've either brought into our marriages or developed within them, it's time to go deeper—to pray against any generational curses that could hinder our families and future generations. This is not just about healing for now. It's about legacy. When you committed to God, you also positioned your family for His covenant blessings. Exodus 20:5–6 tells us that God visits the iniquities of the fathers to the third and fourth generation of those who hate Him, but shows mercy to thousands who love Him and keep His commandments.

We often say things like, "It runs in my family," or "I get it from my mama." And while that might be true, it could also be the very thing keeping you from walking into the fullness of your God-ordained destiny. God wants to bless us and our seed—but we must release the habits, behaviors, and cycles passed down through our bloodlines. Things like a quick temper, abandonment, destructive health patterns, addiction, or breaking the law—these aren't just bad habits. They can be spiritual strongholds that we've been conditioned to accept. And if they've affected you, they will affect those looking up to you—unless you break them.

2 Corinthians 10:4–5 tells us that the weapons we fight with are not carnal but mighty through God for pulling down strongholds. These are spiritual battles, and they require spiritual tools. The battle starts in the mind. When we receive Christ, we become new creatures (2 Corinthians 5:17). That newness comes with power over every past behavior that once held us captive.

We can form new patterns and begin new mindsets by breaking curses—but first, we have to identify them. Maybe you've struggled with negativity that seems generational. Maybe it's addiction, anxiety, or even a recurring pattern of infidelity or divorce. If you don't know what's lurking in your bloodline, ask God to reveal it. He is light, and in Him there is no darkness (1 John 1:5). And since we are His children, we must walk in that light (John 8:12).

You may need to fast to hear God clearly and be free from distraction. Ask the Holy Spirit to guide your fast—what to fast from, what to fast for, and how long to do it.

Please understand: this process is not optional. It is crucial—mandatory, even. If we don't expose and confront these generational issues, we risk passing them down. God *wants* our bloodline to be blessed, prosperous, and free.

Prayer

Lord, I understand that there are spiritual battles I can't see, and I acknowledge that there may be generational curses affecting my family line. I ask You to reveal those patterns to me and give me the spiritual wisdom and strength I need to break them through Your power. In Jesus' name, Amen.

The Vow Within

I vow to stand in the gap for my bloodline. What has plagued generations before me ends with me—by the power and authority of Jesus Christ.

Reflections

Use the space below to write what God reveals to you through fasting, prayer, and intentional seeking. What generational patterns must be broken to protect your marriage, your family, and your future?

____

____

____

____

Seventeen

Praying for Deliverance and Freedom

"If the Son therefore shall make you free, ye shall be free indeed." —John 8:36 KJV

Now that God has revealed the generational curses affecting your life and bloodline, it's time to go to war in prayer—declaring deliverance and walking in the freedom Christ already secured for you. But it begins with a repentant heart.

Acts 3:19 reminds us that there is restoration in repentance. When we repent, we're not only seeking forgiveness for ourselves—we're standing in the gap for our entire bloodline. We're declaring to the enemy: *It stops with me.* The past does not define who we are in Christ. Romans 8:1 assures us that there is no condemnation for those who are in Him. God's grace is greater than any family cycle, pattern, or curse. His blood cleanses and makes us new.

After repentance, renounce every demonic covenant or agreement that may have been made—knowingly or unknowingly—in your family line. Ask God to cleanse and deliver your bloodline, believing that what you pray, you will receive. There is no room for doubt. Mark 11:25 teaches that we must ask in faith, without wavering, if we want to receive anything from the Lord.

Pray with power. Pray with authority. Cast down every lie and ounce of shame the enemy has tried to plant in your mind to keep you feeling bound. God has given you the authority to tread on serpents and over *all* the power of the enemy—and nothing shall harm you (Luke 10:19).

Ask the Lord to break every ungodly covenant and replace it with a new, holy covenant with Him. Cover your spouse, your children, and generations yet unborn. Ezekiel 18:20 gives us hope: the righteous will not bear the punishment of the wicked. Through Christ, your bloodline is made new.

When temptation comes, when old ways try to creep back in, when you feel like going backward—remember the promises of God. Declare them over your life. Meditate on these scriptures:

- *I sought the Lord, and He heard me, and delivered me from all my fears.* — Psalm 34:4

- *Many are the afflictions of the righteous, but the Lord delivers him out of them all.* — Psalm 34:19

- *Stand fast in the liberty by which Christ has made us free, and do not be entangled again with a yoke of bondage...but through love serve one another.* — Galatians 5:1,13

- *Where the Spirit of the Lord is, there is liberty.* — 2 Corinthians 3:17
- *You shall know the truth, and the truth shall make you free.* — John 8:32
- *He is able also to save to the uttermost those who come to God through Him, since He always lives to make intercession for them.* — Hebrews 7:25

Believe that you and your family are free. Walk in that freedom boldly. And don't forget to thank Him for it!

Prayer

God, thank You for revealing the generational strongholds in my life. Help me to renounce and break them so my bloodline may be made whole. I ask You to replace every ungodly covenant with a holy, lasting covenant with You. Thank You for new freedom. Continue to strengthen me when I feel weak or tempted to go backward. In Jesus' name, Amen.

The Vow Within

I vow to walk in the freedom Christ died to give me. I will not return to the bondage I've been delivered from. My bloodline is cleansed, my future is redeemed, and my family is free.

Reflections

Congratulations on your freedom! How do you feel? What does this freedom look like in your everyday life? Record your thoughts and give God praise for the victory.

Eighteen

Full Restoration: How God Restores

"And I will restore to you the years that the locust hath eaten, the cankerworm, and the caterpiller, and the palmerworm, my great army which I sent among you."
—Joel 2:25 KJV

When God moves, He doesn't do things halfway. That includes restoration. To restore something means to bring it back to its original state—fully, completely, and without lack.

In 1 Samuel 30, David and his soldiers return to Ziklag—a city where David, his family, and the families of his men lived while he was being hunted by Saul. But instead of home, they're met with devastation. The city was burned to the ground. Their wives, children, and possessions were all gone. Scripture says they cried until they had no strength left. Yet somehow, they still had enough strength to want to stone David, blaming him for what had happened because they were following his orders. But that's a sermon for another book!

Understandably, David was distressed. But then something powerful happened: "David encouraged himself in the Lord." I'm always encouraged by that verse. Because even in our lowest moments, we are never too weak for God to lift us up. (But that's a sermon for another day too!)

David inquired of God: should he pursue the enemy? God answered, yes—pursue them, and without fail, you will recover all.

In their moment of grief, they had no idea that God was already orchestrating restoration. And sometimes, neither do we. Maybe you're not grieving the physical loss of your spouse—but it feels like you're grieving your marriage. You're not as close as you once were. You can't imagine reconciliation. It seems like hope is slipping through your fingers.

But hear me: hopelessness doesn't come from God. It's a lie from the enemy meant to rob you of faith. When hope feels distant, return to the Word:

- *Psalm 25:21* — "I wait on Thee."
- *Psalm 39:7* — "And so, Lord, where do I put my hope? My only hope is in You."
- *Psalm 33:22* — "Let Your mercy be upon us, O Lord, according as we hope in You."
- *Psalm 71:5* — "For You are my hope, O Lord."

If God said your marriage can be restored, then restoration is possible. Numbers 23:19 reminds us that God is not a man that He should lie. Whatever God speaks, He makes good!

Reclaim what the enemy is trying to destroy. Speak life into your marriage—declare it blessed, unified, and founded on Christ. Don't let the ashes convince you that resurrection isn't possible. In Lamentations 5:21, they cried, "Restore us, O Lord, and bring us back to You again! Give us back the joys we once had!" Yes—your marriage can be joyous again. Not just restored, but renewed.

My favorite verse in the story of David's recovery is verse 19: "And they lacked nothing." They didn't just get back what was lost—they had everything they needed. That's what God does when He restores. No residue. No lack. Just fullness.

Everything you need for a healthy, thriving marriage is in Christ. In His presence is fullness of joy (Psalm 16:11). He is not a respecter of persons. What He's done for others, He will do for you. The circumstances may differ, but the promises remain.

Prayer

God, thank You for Your kindness in giving me promises concerning my marriage. I'm only here because You've kept me. And if You haven't released me, then You're still doing something in my marriage. Strengthen my faith to trust Your Word, for You are a covenant-keeping God. I give my marriage to You, knowing that You can reconcile and restore all. I declare healing, unity, and peace. You are our foundation, and I thank You for the victory in advance. In Jesus' name, Amen.

The Vow Within

I vow to believe God's Word over my circumstances. I trust that what was lost can be restored, and what was broken can be rebuilt.

Reflections

If you heard God speak to you today, what is He saying about your marriage, your hope, or your next step? Write it down and hold fast to it.

____

____

____

____

____

____

____

____

____

____

____

____

____

Nineteen

Praying For Our Children

"Train up a child in the way he should go: and when he is old, he will not depart from it." — Proverbs 22:6 KJV

Our children are a blessing from God, no matter how much they try us. In Psalm 127:3, children are called a heritage—a prized possession to God. He loves them more than we ever could. He created them for us and entrusted them to us. They are our legacy, but they are God's first. They are an extension of us in this world, so what we teach them matters. Whether they are yours through conception, adoption, or marriage, parenting is a holy and life-changing opportunity given by God to steward them well—teaching them about His ways so they can be used for His kingdom. You should want your child to have a deep relationship with God, a steadfast faith in Him, and to know the joy that comes from walking with Him daily.

But maybe your journey of being unequally yoked is taking a toll on them. Maybe they're witnessing arguments and disagreements between you and your spouse, and it's affecting them. Perhaps they're acting out, refusing to go to church with you. Their attitude has changed, they're disrespectful, their grades have dropped. Nothing you do or say is getting through to them, and you don't know what else to do.

Or maybe your child isn't showing signs of rebellion. They're doing well in school, involved in church, and active in extracurricular activities. Regardless of the season they're in—when we pray, we are covering them.

Prayer is one of the most powerful ways we can protect our kids. When we notice behavioral changes, interceding for them should be our first response. Covering our children in prayer across every area of their lives is one of the greatest acts of stewardship we can offer. We've seen how prayer has changed our lives—it can do the same for the ones God has entrusted to us.

Not sure what to pray for? Ask God to open their hearts to you, revealing what they may be afraid or unwilling to share. Pray that God would open their eyes to His truth so they may walk in His freedom and love. Ask God to wrap His arms around them in times of loneliness and despair. When they face difficult decisions, pray that God will guide them. Pray that their hearts remain tender—toward you, toward your spouse, and especially toward God. Pray for their salvation and that they will remain in Christ.

Praying *with* our children builds their confidence to pray for themselves. As you pray with them, include your spouse in those prayers. Invite your child to pray aloud about what's on their heart concerning their parent. Agree with them in prayer for their parent's salvation and deliverance. When those prayers are answered, not only will your faith grow, but theirs will too. The example of prayer we set now will sustain them through this season—and every season to come.

Prayer

Heavenly Father, let our children walk in Your ways. Break every curse, and let their lives reflect Your goodness. I pray that our united prayers for my spouse will be answered, and that our children's faith in You will increase. In Jesus' name, Amen.

The Vow Within

I vow to cover my children in prayer—daily, intentionally, and with faith that God will shape their hearts and their future.

Reflections

How has this journey of being unequally yoked affected your child(ren)? Have they revealed anything to you that they want to pray about concerning their parent?

____

____

____

____

Twenty

We Are On the Same Team

"For our struggle is not against flesh and blood, but against the rulers, against the authorities, against the powers of this dark world." — Ephesians 6:12 KJV

No matter what your spouse's faith is, you are on the same team. You both took vows to stay committed through good times and bad, in sickness and in health. You may not have specifically vowed to stay together through differing beliefs, but that commitment still stands—spoken or not. God is a covenant-keeping God, and He expects us to be the same—until He releases us from our marriages.

Sometimes, it may feel like your spouse is the enemy, especially when they don't believe what you believe. But you still have a responsibility to cultivate and grow together. Maybe you have children, maybe you run a business together—whatever it is, the blessings that flow through your marriage are connected to you.

Because your spouse is not walking in God's perfect will, it can be difficult to fight alongside them against the real enemy. So, what are some practical ways you can show unity in your marriage?

There are natural tools you can use to build cohesion despite spiritual differences. If communication is an issue, find ways to grow in that area together. Listen to marriage podcasts. Seek couples or individual therapy. Try communication exercises or games. Speak more clearly and provide extra context if needed.

If either of you feels neglected, address it. Listen intently when your spouse shares. Spend quality time together—put the devices down and be present. If *you* feel neglected, express your needs, and give your spouse room to process before re-engaging. Help more around the house. Plan regular alone time. Go on dates. Take vacations.

These natural steps matter even as you war spiritually for their salvation. Remember, faith without works is dead (James 2:20). You can't expect God to move in their heart while you're mistreating them. Their eternal soul matters now. If you're newly saved, don't neglect your duties as a spouse because of your zeal for Jesus. God still calls you to serve them, even in their unbelief.

Don't stop loving your spouse because they don't believe what you believe. You are on the same team—and this team is a winning team.

Prayer

God, help me to remember that although my spouse may not be saved, I still have a commitment to love and honor them. Give us tools to fight naturally as I fight spiritually. I believe they will come to know You as their Lord and Savior. Help me to continue loving them, even through our differences. Amen.

The Vow Within

I vow to fight for unity in my marriage, knowing that the real enemy is not my spouse. We are one team, and through Christ, we win.

Reflections

What are some things you're facing in your marriage right now? What natural or spiritual tools can you use to address them?

____

____

____

____

____

____

____

____

Twenty-One

Don't Act Like That

"But be ye doers of the word, and not hearers only, deceiving your own selves." —James 1:22 KJV

Let's be honest—how we treat our unbelieving spouses speaks louder than any Scripture we can quote. John 13:35 reminds us that it is by our love—not our arguments or even our convictions—that others will know we are His disciples. Faith and actions must walk hand-in-hand.

To love someone is to actively show affection, grace, and value toward them—especially when it's difficult. This love should not be conditional, reserved only for good days or when they meet our expectations. So how do we rise above our emotional responses? We look to the Father.

We quote John 3:16 so often, but do we live it? God gave His sinless Son to die for a sinful world. He endured humiliation, pain, and rejection to save people who would never say thank you—people who would never love Him back. That kind of love is not only sacrificial, it's supernatural. And it is the very love we are called to reflect in our homes.

Clinical psychologists John and Julie Gottman found that kindness is the single most important factor for a satisfying marriage. Scripture confirms this. 1 Corinthians 13:4 says, "Love suffers long and is kind." In Greek, *makrothumia* (longsuffering) means enduring with passion, and *chrēstos* (kind) means intentional grace. The revelation? Love remains kind even through suffering.

Jesus, hanging on the cross in agony, cried out, "Father, forgive them." No conditions. No expectations. Just love. Would we do the same for our spouses—especially when they don't reciprocate?

Our flesh fights this. Pride tells us not to love unless we're loved back. But Christ loved knowing many would reject Him. That's our model.

So, what if we adopted that mindset? What if, instead of reacting out of frustration, we paused to pray for our spouse's healing? What if we chose kindness in the moments where it felt hardest? Romans 2:4 says it was God's kindness that led us to repentance. That same kindness can soften even the hardest heart. The process isn't instant. It may take weeks, months, or years. You'll likely stumble—yell, shut down, say something you regret. But grace is available. Forgiveness is possible.

James 1:22 warns us: Don't just listen to the Word—live it. Transformation begins when we hide the Word in our hearts (Psalm 119:11), forgive quickly, and lean on the Holy Spirit for help. Lean into the Word. Let it reshape your heart. Practice kindness even when it's inconvenient. Rehearse *2 Peter 1:7*, *Isaiah 40:31*, and *Colossians 3:23-24*—verses that remind us that what we do in private matters more than what others see. Neuroscience shows it takes over 60 days to form a habit. But with the Spirit's help, your timeline may be shorter. The more you practice grace, the more it becomes your default. Let your life preach louder than your lips. Let your actions show Christ's dominion over your heart. Change is a process, not a one-time decision. And that God honors the unseen sacrifices of obedience.

Let your conduct speak louder than your complaints. Your spouse may not remember every Scripture you quote—but they'll remember how you made them feel. So, choose love. Every time.

Prayer

Lord, forgive me for the moments when I failed to reflect Your love to my spouse. Help me to show kindness, even through discomfort. Help me to love with a sacrificial heart, even when I feel unseen or unappreciated. Teach me to love with no strings attached, just like You did. Give me the strength to be a doer of Your Word—not just in public, but in private too. Teach me to reflect Your kindness, to die to my flesh, and to serve in love—not for recognition, but as worship unto You. In Jesus name, Amen.

The Vow Within

Love is more than a feeling—it's a reflection of Christ in action. Today, I vow to be mindful of how I speak to and treat my spouse, not based on how I feel, but rooted in who God has called me to be.

I choose grace over grudge, patience over pride, and compassion over convenience. Even when I feel unseen or misunderstood, I will reflect the love of Christ through my actions. Because love is not just spoken—it's lived.

Reflections

In what ways have I allowed frustration, silence, or sharp words to replace love in action? What is one intentional act of Christlike love I can show my spouse today, regardless of how they respond? Write it down—and do it.

____

____

____

____

____

____

____

____

____

____

____

____

____

____

____

Twenty-Two

Praying for Wisdom and Understanding

If any of you lack wisdom, let him ask of God, that giveth to all men liberally, and upbraideth not; and it shall be given him. —*James 1:5 KJV*

Throughout my marriage journey, I oftentimes felt helpless—like I just couldn't get a read on my husband. It often seemed that nothing I did was ever good enough. If he asked me to be mindful of something that bothered him, I would adjust because I wanted him to feel heard. But more often than not, what seemed like a big deal one day wouldn't matter to him the next. I would pour time, money, and effort into something, only to be let down again. Over and over, I found myself in the same cycle—frustrated and exhausted. I didn't know how to get out, and I needed help.

Maybe this sounds familiar to you. You've done all you know to do. You've communicated until you're blue in the face, and now, you're all talked out. Marriage already comes with its challenges, and being unequally yoked can multiply those challenges tenfold.

Simple disagreements turn into explosive arguments. Small offenses feel magnified by the spiritual disconnect, and over time, hopelessness creeps in.

But there's hope. In moments like these, we must go to God for help in understanding our spouse. Job 28 reminds us that wisdom isn't found in the earth or sky—it must be sought from the One who created all. The best advice we will ever receive will always come from our Creator. God knows our spouses, our marriages, and our situations intimately. He is a good Father who longs to give generously when we ask.

James 1:5 is clear: if we lack wisdom, we must ask for it. But with wisdom must come obedience (Psalm 19:7). When God answers, we have a responsibility to obey. It's foolish to ask for insight and then ignore the instruction. God's wisdom is a constant guide for every part of our lives—including our marriages (Psalm 119:98).

Proverbs 4:7 says, "Wisdom is the principal thing; therefore, get wisdom. And with all your getting, get understanding." It's not enough to receive divine wisdom—we also need understanding to know how to apply it. Ask the Lord to make the application clear. Seek godly counsel (Proverbs 1:5) and surround yourself with resources that can speak to your specific circumstances.

In Proverbs 31, a wise woman is called virtuous. She speaks with kindness, and her husband trusts her to do him no harm. Wives, wisdom and gentleness can disarm even the most defensive spouse. This virtuous woman fears the Lord and obeys His voice. She begins with examining herself and shifts her approach accordingly.

Men, Ephesians 5:28 offers wisdom on how to love your wife—by loving her as your own body. Speak words of kindness that soothe, not provoke (Proverbs 15:1). Let tenderness shape your tone and presence. Husbands and wives alike, choose to ask—not demand. Speak with the same love you hope to receive.

God promises that when we seek Him, He pours out His Spirit, makes His Word known, and increases our wisdom (Proverbs 1:23). But we must seek Him. We must lean into His Word, listen closely to His wisdom, and allow understanding to shape our response.

Prayer

God, I thank You for the wisdom and understanding You freely give. Help me to apply what You reveal in ways that honor my spouse and reflect Your heart. Teach me how to better understand them, and give me discernment in every decision. Amen.

The Vow Within

I vow to seek God first when I don't understand my spouse. I will pursue wisdom, and I will follow through with obedience.

Reflections

In what areas are you seeking wisdom for your marriage? What has God revealed to you today to help you walk out this journey with grace and understanding?

Twenty-Three
Daily Bread

"Give us this day our daily bread." — Matthew 6:11 KJV

There's a hymn I used to love hearing the deacons sing growing up—particularly Pop Baker and Deacon Alston. They had such beautiful vibrato, it was almost as if when they sang, velvet erupted out of them. You could tell they truly believed every lyric. The hymn is called *I Need Thee Every Hour* by Annie Hawks. Some would assume it was written from a place of desperation or a cry for help. But in truth, it was written from a place of joy and love for the Lord. Annie knew that without Christ, she was nothing—and she fully depended on the One who gave her life.

In today's society, we're always seeking something to give us temporary happiness—clothes, cars, houses, money. But with all our seeking, are we seeking God? When it comes to your marriage, are you pursuing God for help, or are you just winging it to get through the day? Are we squeezing Him into our schedules with five-minute devotionals, or are we carving out meaningful time to sit with Him? Does He get your attention before social media does? Is the only time He hears from you when things are going wrong? Is God your first resort—or your last?

I'm sure when you first got saved, your passion made you feel like you could slay Goliath. You were deeply connected to the Savior and wanted to know everything about Him. But somewhere along the road, that fondness faded, and the distractions of life set in. That's because salvation is just the beginning of pursuing Christ. He wants us to seek Him *daily*. He wants to talk to you every day—just like a spouse would. After all, we are His bride.

In every aspect of our lives—spiritual, financial, emotional, and marital—we must diligently pursue God. Hebrews 11:6 tells us that He rewards those who continually seek Him. But let the reward not be our motive. We seek Him to know Him intimately. Because with intimacy comes strength and joy (Psalm 105:3–4)—strength to endure hard times in our marriage, and joy to sustain us when our union brings sorrow. Quality time with God grows our faith and strengthens our relationship with Him. We must never grow content in our relationship with God; we must be in constant pursuit of His heart.

Seek God for guidance in your marriage. Seek Him confidently in every area of life. If there are financial concerns, consult His Word and ask for wisdom. Need help responding better to your spouse? Scripture speaks to that too. Ask Him to help you love your spouse like He loves us. Struggling with intimacy? The *Song of Solomon* has wisdom. Facing mental and emotional battles that are affecting your marriage? Pray for emotional regulation and a sound mind.

God wants us to chase after Him because He *is* the answer to every problem we have. He created us—and He created marriage. Nothing is too hard or too big for Him to move on our behalf. But we must commune with Him.

The next time there's a disagreement or offense in your marriage, resist the urge to vent on social media. Those folks don't need to know your business. (Whew, chile—this convicted me as I'm typing it!) Before you run to YouTube looking for answers to the same issues that keep resurfacing in your marriage, run to God first. He may still lead you to a helpful video, but only after He's filtered out the noise that caters to your flesh.

Remember—God cares about your marriage because He created it. And the Creator knows *all* and *is* all. Seek Him first, and all His righteousness will be added unto you—including in your marriage.

Prayer

God, thank You for the opportunity to draw closer to You with each new day. You grant us fresh mercies daily, so I will seek You daily. Help me to look to You first for guidance in my marriage because You are the Author and Finisher. Amen.

The Vow Within

I vow to pursue God daily for wisdom, strength, and joy—trusting that in knowing Him, I will find what I need for my marriage.

Reflections

In what ways are you not putting God first? How can you better pursue Him each day?

Twenty-Four

Anointing Your Home

"And if it seem evil unto you to serve the Lord, choose you this day whom ye will serve; whether the gods which your fathers served that were on the other side of the flood, or the gods of the Amorites, in whose land ye dwell: but as for me and my house, we will serve the Lord." —*Joshua 24:15 KJV*

If I can be completely honest, this scripture was hard for me to believe for a long time. Growing up, we went to church, but not everyone in my home was saved. And then there's my marriage. Living with a spouse who doesn't believe in God made this verse feel almost irrelevant—like it could never apply to me. Have you ever felt that way? That the hope of your spouse serving God seems bleak? That there's no light at the end of the tunnel? If so, it may be time to pull out the oil!

Throughout the Bible, oil was used to anoint, heal, and cleanse. 2 Corinthians 7:1 urges us to cleanse ourselves from unholy thoughts and actions. But what does it mean to *cleanse*? According to Merriam-Webster, as a verb, it means "to make thoroughly clean." As a noun, it refers to "a process of ridding the body of substances regarded as toxins."

In Exodus 30:23–25, God instructed Moses to mix specific spices with oil to anoint the tabernacle and consecrate Aaron and his sons as priests. In James 5, the elders anointed the sick with oil while praying for their healing. When we accepted Christ, we were cleansed from our sins by a liquid—the blood He shed on Calvary. Just as our bodies were made clean, our homes—dwelling places—must also be consecrated. Demons will try to inhabit any place they can. But God's power is stronger.

So, how do we anoint our homes and set them apart for God? Start by taking some oil and praying over it. Ask God to make it holy and use it for His glory. Then go in! Anoint your bed and any others, praying protection as your household sleeps and rebuking any demonic attack. Pray over the people in your home—that they would walk in holiness and serve the Lord. Anoint your kitchen and everything in it, praying over the food you prepare and consume. Go to the entryways, commanding unclean spirits to leave and never return. Anoint devices, praying they won't be used for unrighteousness or lewd behavior. Anoint whatever the Lord leads you to. Be obedient.

You may see dysfunction and disunity in your home today. But don't let that discourage you. When we consecrate our homes to God, we are inviting His presence and blessing. His blood, like the oil, is powerful enough to cleanse even the most wayward heart. He can sanctify your marriage and restore unity in your home.

Psalm 133 beautifully describes unity among God's people. David likens it to precious oil flowing from Aaron's head down to his garments—an anointing that released an aroma pleasing to God. Where there is unity, God commands a blessing. That's the promise. And God is able.

Prayer

Thank You, God, for the symbol of oil and its power throughout Your Word. I pray that You would consecrate our home and our marriage. May everyone who dwells here serve You with their whole heart. Let Your presence rest here and let every inch of our home and marriage be set apart for Your glory. In Jesus' name, Amen.

The Vow Within

I vow to cover my household with prayer and obedience. I declare this house will serve the Lord, and I will actively consecrate this space as holy ground.

Reflections

Ask God to reveal to you the areas of your home that need to be sanctified with oil. What is He telling you to pray for?

Twenty-Five

Spiritual Warfare

"For the weapons of our warfare are not carnal, but mighty through God to the pulling down of strong holds;" — 2 Corinthians 10:4 KJV

In order for us to be effective as Christians in our marriages, we must first understand that we are in a spiritual war—a battle between flesh and spirit. As soldiers in this war, we need to be equipped with both defensive and offensive weapons. We must be well-trained and well-armed to win, knowing who our enemy is and who our God is.

One of Satan's tactics is to twist God's Word just enough to make it sound believable, planting seeds of doubt about the Word-giver Himself. That's why it's imperative that we know God's voice—and know it well—so we won't be deceived by another (John 10:4–5). When Satan tempted Jesus in the wilderness by quoting Scripture (Matthew 4:4; Luke 4:4), Jesus resisted by quoting the Word back. He *is* the Living Word—so the Word was already hidden in His heart. We must also partake of the Word daily if we want to win daily (Psalm 119:11).

Satan wants nothing more than to destroy your marriage by killing your faith—whether through doubt, discouragement, or outright deception. He attacks with suggestive temptation and blatant lies meant to confuse us (Genesis 3). To combat this, we must pray, rebuke, and resist the enemy, while submitting our minds to God so that the devil will flee (James 4:7). Spiritual warfare strengthens both our faith in God and our defense against the enemy. To endure, we will be tested—but every time we resist the enemy, we become more aware of his tactics.

Ephesians 6:10–17 is a well-known passage because it outlines the *whole* armor of God. This armor is spiritual protection—used to fight against demonic activity, not against our spouses. It is called the *whole* armor because it guards the mind, body, and spirit in totality, just like a knight's armor protects every part of the body. If there's a weak spot, the enemy will target it. That's why the armor must be complete. We can't afford to engage in battle without it—because without it, we'll lose every time. Verse 11 instructs us to put on the armor so we can stand against Satan's schemes. Even the conversations that used to end in arguments can now be seasoned with peace—because we've chosen to walk in peace.

To win, we must shift our mindset about the battles we face. 2 Timothy 2:3 encourages us to endure hardship like a good soldier—knowing that our suffering is for the glory of God. We don't fight just to fight. God promises blessings to those who hold fast to their faith. James 1:12 calls those who endure temptation *blessed* and assures us of the crown of life. James 5:11 says those who endure are *happy*. Just like a mother must endure labor pains to birth something beautiful, we too must endure challenges to receive God's promises for our marriages.

The Word is our greatest offensive weapon—because it's alive, powerful, and sharper than any two-edged sword. It's our shield, our defense, and our strategy. Speak the Word against every lie Satan tells you about your marriage. Speak blessings from Scripture and rebuke every curse. Remember, armor is not for the weak. It's heavy and hard to carry at first. But with practice comes strength, and with use comes victory. Ask God for strength, because this battle isn't ours—it's His. And He's already guaranteed the victory. Go forth and win!

Prayer

God, thank You for the ability to fight. Thank You for equipping me with armor to defeat the real enemy in my marriage. I pray that You give me the strength to fight when I feel weak. Equip me with the right tactics to use and teach me when to use them. In Jesus' name, Amen.

The Vow Within

I vow to suit up daily in the full armor of God—to guard my mind, my heart, and my home. I vow to fight the real enemy, not my spouse, and to walk in the authority and truth of God's Word. I vow to speak life over my marriage, to wield the sword of the

Spirit with boldness, and to remain watchful and prayerful. I vow to stand firm in faith, even when it's hard, because the battle is not mine—it's the Lord's.

Reflections

What piece of the armor do you need to put on—or strengthen? How will this positively impact your marriage?

Twenty-Six
Think Bigger Picture

"Who against hope believed in hope, that he might become the father of many nations, according to that which was spoken, So shall thy seed be." — Romans 4:18 KJV

I love the story of Abraham. I really do. Growing up in church, I had heard his story many times but never paid much attention to it. One day, I decided to read the story of Abraham as a fully grown adult. I was on the metro on my way to church, reading my Bible, when I came across the passage where Sarai tells Abram to sleep with Hagar. I was so confused! Like, did she really just give a hall pass to her husband?! *And he took it!* That's when I realized—even some of the strongest people can have the weakest moments and take their eyes off the promises of God.

So how is Abraham written in the hall of faith in Romans and Hebrews? Because his story didn't end with the mistake of getting Hagar pregnant with Ishmael. God appeared to Abram again and changed his name to Abraham, reaffirming and establishing the promise He had spoken over him. That encounter boosted Abraham's faith. He not only received the promised child, Isaac, but he was also willing to sacrifice him in obedience to God.

I can't help but wonder how confused Abraham must have been, knowing that God had made an everlasting covenant with the very child He was now telling him to sacrifice. Did Abraham believe God was contradicting Himself? Or maybe Abraham saw the bigger picture. Maybe deep down he trusted the One who had always proved faithful—who had always performed what He promised.

In the midst of everyday life—the ups and downs, the good and bad—it's easy to take our eyes off the prize. It's tempting to wonder, *What's the point of all this trying? What am I still doing here?* The answer is simple: God has called you to this walk because He knows you're capable of seeing it through. He has entrusted you with this delicate gift—this precious opportunity to stand in the gap for your spouse and, in many cases, your children. God doesn't call the incapable; He equips the called with His strength and power.

The problem is, we often look at our situation through our own flawed lenses. And when we do, it scares us. Our vision becomes distorted. We no longer see the light at the end of the tunnel.

Hebrews 12:1–3 encourages us to:

- Remember that there are people rooting for us when we can't root for ourselves.

- Keep our eyes on Jesus, the Author and Finisher of our

faith—because He sees the end from the beginning.

- Know that Jesus endured the cross, keeping the big picture in mind, and is now seated in victory. If Jesus could endure the physical cross, surely we can endure a spiritual one.

So, what are some ways that we can stay focused on the bigger picture?

Believe that what God has promised will come to pass.

- Numbers 23:19
- Psalm 89:34–35; 110:4
- Malachi 3:6

Eliminate all negative thoughts and speech that deter belief.

- 2 Corinthians 10:5
- Psalm 139:23; 19:14; 51:10

Obey what He has told you.

- Philippians 2:13
- John 14:15–17

Remember: God entrusted you with this assignment because He knows you're strong and capable. Keep your eyes fixed on what He has spoken over your marriage. Shift your perspective—because if you believe it's a lost cause, it will be. But if you continue to believe in His promises, you will receive the reward.

Prayer

God, thank You for helping me focus on the promise instead of the problem. Teach me to see beyond my circumstances and keep my eyes on what You've spoken. Strengthen my faith to trust You in all things. In Jesus' name, Amen.

The Vow Within

I vow to keep my eyes on the promise, not the problem. I will not allow discouragement or delay to convince me otherwise. I will trust in what You said, Lord—even when I don't understand it. I will believe that You are faithful and able to do just what You said You would do.

Reflections

How have you taken your eyes off the bigger picture? How can you regain your focus?

____

____

____

____

____

Twenty-Seven

Waiting Well

"If a man die, shall he live again? all the days of my appointed time will I wait, till my change come." —Job 14:14 KJV

A family sits, anxious to hear the news of their loved one's condition. Worry and anxiety fuel their thoughts. But in the midst of the unknown, they decide to gather. Holding hands, they pray, seeking God's face for strength and peace in this difficult moment. They are in the waiting room.

Maybe you can't relate to this family in this specific experience, but you, my friend, are in a waiting room. You're anticipating a move from God in your marriage concerning the salvation of your spouse. You've received a word from the Lord—a prophecy, a dream, a vision—something that has yet to manifest. It hasn't come to pass, and you don't know how much longer you can wait. You're ready to walk away. It doesn't seem worth it anymore.

Waiting is a part of life—a requirement in the journey of trusting God. Page after page, chapter after chapter, God's people were taught to wait on the promises spoken over them. Noah and the

So instead of throwing in the towel, lift your eyes to the hills (Psalm 121:1). God hasn't just given us His Word—He's given us His Spirit. That's a divine advantage. Ask Him for what you need to endure to the end.

Are you weary? Isaiah 40:31 and Psalm 27:14 promise renewed strength in the waiting. Draw closer to Him and He will draw near to you. He wants to meet you in your doubts and prove them wrong.

Wait and be patient. Rest in His promises (Psalm 37:7). He always keeps His Word. There's no need to worry whether something will come to pass if He's already spoken it. Wait patiently, and He will hear you (Psalm 40:1). Continue to trust in His Word (Psalm 130:5).

Speak the outcome. Your words have power. If God has promised it, it *will* happen. Speak the truth so you can believe the truth.

Worship while you wait. Deny the pity party and choose to worship. This is how you tell God you believe His Word. He's worthy in the waiting and when the waiting is over.

God redeems in the waiting. There is not one story where God asked someone to wait in vain. He declared a thing—and He brought it to pass. Ask Sarah. Ask Job. Ask Noah. Ask Joseph. Just you wait—your name is next.

Prayer

God, thank You for the gift that is waiting. Help me to see it as a blessing and not a burden. Draw patience and contentment out of me so I can wait well—believing that what You say about my marriage will, indeed, come to pass.

The Vow Within

I vow to trust in the promises God has spoken over my marriage, even when the wait feels long and uncertain. I will not let doubt speak louder than His Word. I will wait with a posture of faith, not frustration—with worship, not worry. I vow to seek God's presence over His promises and to allow Him to strengthen me in the waiting. I believe that what He has spoken, He will bring to pass.

Reflections

What has God said about your marriage? Do you believe it? Why or why not? Where does your faith need to be strengthened?

____

____

____

____

____

Twenty-Eight
The Company We Keep

"A friend loveth at all times, and a brother is born for adversity." — Proverbs 17:17 KJV

In this season of waiting, our village is a vital part of our endurance. Who we surround ourselves with can determine whether we sink or swim, believe or doubt what God has said. In times of adversity and hardship, we need good, godly support—people who hear from God and will lift us up when we're too weak to stand on our own.

In Exodus 17, the people of Israel fought against Amalek while Moses, Hur, and Aaron stood on a hill and watched. Every time Moses held up his hands, Israel would prosper. But when his hands fell, they began to lose. So, Aaron and Hur put a stone under him to sit on and each held up one of his arms—ensuring that Israel prevailed. Catch this: although Moses was resting on the Rock, he still needed godly support beside him to ensure the victory!

God, as a compassionate Father, comforts us through His Holy Spirit, but He goes the extra mile by surrounding us with people to walk through life with. In Genesis 2, God told Adam that it wasn't good for man to be alone. This principle doesn't just apply to marriage—it applies to community. David and Jonathan shared a covenant bond of true friendship, even when Jonathan's father hated David. They understood the power of godly connection.

The wrong relationships, though, can lead us in the wrong direction. Consider the prophet in 1 Kings 13 who was given strict instructions by God not to eat or drink or return the way he came. While resting, an older prophet lied and told him an angel said it was fine to come back with him and eat. The younger prophet believed him and disobeyed God. The same lying prophet then gave him a word of judgment from the Lord—and the younger prophet died soon after. That's wild! The very person who deceived him confirmed the punishment for disobedience. While most relationships won't result in physical death, some can cause spiritual decay if they draw you away from the Word God has spoken over you.

Proverbs 12:26 says the righteous choose their friends carefully. Psalm 1:1 tells us the blessed person does not walk in the counsel of the ungodly. So, what if they go to church? If their advice contradicts what you know God has spoken, they are not walking in godly wisdom. No one who is aligned with Christ will encourage you to disobey the voice of God. Don't let Satan use negative or even well-meaning voices to pull you off course.

Surround yourself with godly, likeminded people—mentors, couples, and friends—who can pour into you when your cup is low. Seek out those who will share testimonies, offer flood. Sarah and Hannah with their babies. Job losing his entire family and livestock. While waiting is difficult, if you hold on, it will be worth it.

Waiting on God requires the right heart and mind posture. The Hebrew word for "wait" is *qavah*, which means to bind together. In waiting, we become vulnerable to the Father. This place of spiritual nakedness is designed to draw us closer to Him—intertwining our hopes, desires, and will with His. Every opportunity for intimacy with God in this season should be seized, so you don't faint.

Sometimes the reason you feel like giving up is because you're focused more on the promise than the Promise Keeper. You may have received a prophecy about your spouse's salvation, and now you're hyper-fixated on its fulfillment. But that word never came with a timestamp. So when circumstances go left, it makes you question what you were told. *Waiting is a test—a mirror that exposes what's truly in your heart, showing you yourself.*

Are you waiting with patience or bitterness? Are you angry that change hasn't come?

Though feelings like frustration and impatience are normal, they can hinder your ability to wait well. If you're only focused on time lost, you'll miss what God is trying to teach you. He's drawing you closer. He's refining you—shaping you into someone who can withstand greater trials in the future. He's building contentment, peace, joy, trust, and discipline in you. Just like childbirth, there's pain and pressure in the waiting—but the reward makes it all worth it.

encouragement, and walk beside you in faith. Allow trusted people into your vulnerable spaces so they know how to pray for you and hold you up when the weight becomes too heavy.

Prayer

God, I am so grateful for the godly company You've placed in my life—those who walk with me in both good and hard times. I ask that You remove every relationship that doesn't honor You or align with Your will for my marriage. Strengthen the bonds that help me hold onto the promises You've spoken.

The Vow Within

I vow to protect my marriage by surrounding it with godly counsel and Christ-centered community. I will be intentional about the voices I allow to speak into my heart and into my relationship. I vow to walk in discernment, releasing any connections that hinder my obedience to God or weaken my commitment to my spouse. I choose to link arms with those who encourage faith, fight with me in prayer, and remind me of God's promises—even when I forget. My marriage will be covered, strengthened, and guarded through wise community and godly influence.

Reflections

How have the people in your circle affected your walk—for better or worse? Ask God to give you discernment and the strength to release any relationships that are damaging your faith and obedience to His Word.

Twenty-Nine

Salvation is a Promise

"And they said, Believe on the Lord Jesus Christ, and thou shalt be saved, and thy house." — Acts 16:31 KJV

Trusting God for your spouse's salvation can seem futile when you're constantly faced with opposition and doubt in what you see in your relationship. These distractions come to blind us and make us lose sight of what's important: your spouse's soul and the sustaining of your marriage. According to 2 Peter 3:9, God doesn't want to see anyone perish by rejecting Him. So please believe that salvation is available to your spouse just as it was to you.

Salvation is a promise, but it is also a choice. Your partner has to want to be saved. There is no amount of coercion, manipulation, or intimidation that can force them into salvation. If that were the case, then God wouldn't be the loving Father that He is, and we would be robots. He gives us free will to choose between life and death (Deuteronomy 30:19). But the choosing must begin with believing in your heart and confessing with your mouth (Romans

10:9). We choose Him because He first chose us. His love is what draws us to His throne, offering a chance to repent and receive His adoption as children of God through faith in Jesus (Galatians 3:26). But we must allow God to do the work in their hearts like only He can. He loves them more than we possibly ever could.

While it may seem like salvation is the furthest thing from your spouse's mind, it is up to us to believe for it anyway. Acts 16:31 says that they *will* be saved. That's a promise you can hold on to. We know that God doesn't and can't lie, but He works according to our faith. If you continue to believe and not doubt, then it will come to pass. Continue to pray for them and over them—fervently. Fast on their behalf. Speak life into them. Be the example of Christ in your home, continuing to shine your light in the midst of the darkness around you. Treat them as if the change has already occurred. Love them regardless.

Salvation is possible.

Prayer

God, I choose to believe for my spouse's salvation. I choose to stand on Your word that me and my household will be saved. I may not know the how or the when, but I know that You are a promise keeper. Give me the strength to endure, being an example of Your light, shining brightly in dark times. In Jesus' name, Amen.

The Vow Within

I vow to stand on the promise of salvation for my household. I vow to be patient, prayerful, and present while God does the work in my spouse's heart. I will love them in truth, model Christ in our home, and trust God's timing above my own. I will not lose hope—I will remain steadfast, knowing that God is able to save, restore, and redeem every heart, including my spouse's.

Reflections

How have conversations with your spouse about their relationship with God gone in the past? Do they get defensive? Are they nonchalant? Have they expressed any past church hurt or trauma surrounding God? Bring these concerns to God, asking Him to open their heart again and change how they see Him.

____

____

____

____

____

____

____

____

____

Thirty

Don't Give Up!

And let us not be weary in well doing: for in due season we shall reap, if we faint not. — Galatians 6:9 KJV

If. One small word with so much weight—a conjunction connecting two conditional clauses. *If this, then that.* It sets a clear expectation: we will reap, *if* we don't give up. It sounds simple on paper, but in life, it feels much harder. This journey can feel excruciating, debilitating, even irritating. We question the hand of God—even after He's proven Himself faithful time and time again. And yet, we still stagger at His promises, ready to throw in the towel.

When God gives clear instructions, it's imperative to obey and move accordingly. Scripture is filled with people who either obeyed and reaped their reward—or disobeyed and missed out. Let's look at a few examples that reveal the power of obedience and the consequences of disobedience:

- Joshua — The Israelites were told to march around the walls of Jericho once a day for six days, then seven times on the seventh day before blowing trumpets and shouting.

I'm sure they were tired, confused, maybe even annoyed by God's seemingly strange instructions. Yet when they obeyed, the walls came down, and victory was theirs. It takes endurance to obey when you can't see the end result.

- Nehemiah — Despite constant opposition, Nehemiah stayed focused on rebuilding the wall. He stayed committed to the assignment, and God blessed the work of his hands.

- Numbers — The Israelites stood at the edge of the Promised Land, surrounded by enemies. Out of fear, they longed to return to Egypt. Their disbelief led to their destruction—and they missed out on the promise.

We often give up just before the breakthrough, just before clarity comes. This kind of spiritual exhaustion can alter the trajectory of your marriage. So, how do you stay the course and not grow weary?

How to Endure in the Waiting

1. **Use testimonies as fuel.** Revelation 12:11 tells us we overcome by the blood of the Lamb and the word of our testimonies.

2. **Surround yourself with Scripture.** Write verses of faith, strength, and endurance. Post them where you'll see them daily.

3. **Sing praises in the storm.** Worship like your spouse is already saved. Let your heart be lifted by songs of hope and breakthrough.

4. **Lean on godly community.** Let others speak truth and hope into you when your strength is low. Discern who God has placed in your corner.

5. **Fast with intention.** Let fasting heighten your spiritual sensitivity. Pray for your spouse's salvation and your marriage's healing.

6. **Pray without ceasing.** Pray in the calm and in the chaos. God sees every sacrifice, every silent prayer, every effort. There is no substitute for intimacy with Him.

7. **Communicate with your spouse.** Don't bottle up your emotions. Speak the truth in love, even if change doesn't happen right away.

Sometimes God does release you from a marriage that no longer honors Him. But never walk away without His leading. If He releases you, He will walk you into the next season. Until then, trust Him with every ounce of faith you have. All things really *do* work together for the good of those who love Him.

Believing God with you,
Capri Lee

Prayer

God, thank You for the promise that in due season, I will reap if I don't faint. Strengthen my spirit, sustain me with Your Word, and surround me with what I need to keep going. Teach me to wait well, walk wisely, and war effectively. I trust You with my spouse, my marriage, and my heart. In Jesus' name, Amen.

The Vow Within

I vow to keep going even when I feel weary. I vow to trust God's timing, not my own. I vow to stay the course, to walk by faith and not by sight, believing that God's Word over my marriage will come to pass—in His way, and in His time.

Reflections

Reflect on a time when you wanted to give up, but God gave you the strength to endure. What did you learn about yourself and about Him in that season? How can you remind yourself of His faithfulness the next time weariness tries to overtake you? Write a letter to your future self, encouraging her to keep going and trust God's perfect timing.

____

____

____

Acknowledgements

I want to thank every person who poured into me, so that I could pour into this book. Your love, encouragement, and belief gave me the strength to keep going.

To **God**—first and always. Thank You for catching me off guard once again—in the shower, no less—and commissioning me to write this devotional. You gave me the words, the vision, and the grace to endure and live out each line You placed on my heart. All glory belongs to You.

To **Brittany Brooks** of **Yosi Publishing**—thank you for being a light throughout this process. Your encouragement, patience, and professionalism made this journey not only achievable but joyful. You believed in this project and nurtured it with excellence. Your smile and your spirit gave me the confidence to finish strong.

To Isiah **"Pastor Stretch" and Idania "Lady I" Tarlton**—thank you for never letting me quit. You covered me in prayer, held me up when I was weak, and reminded me that endurance is possible through Christ. Your support when I shared snippets of what God was giving me reminded me that this message matters.

To **My Jackie**—thank you for pushing me to keep writing and for sending Scriptures when we were believing for the same promises. And thank you for loving me enough to take KJ off my hands for a full day when I was overwhelmed. That single act of kindness helped me breathe again and gave me the strength to keep pouring into this book.

To **Vic and Michea**—our conversations stirred something in me. You helped me see that this assignment wasn't just for me—it's for every couple navigating the tension between belief and breakthrough. Thank you for hyping me up and helping me see the bigger picture.

To **Deacon Bernard and Deaconess Cartia**—thank you for pouring into our marriage through countless counseling sessions, phone calls, texts, and even rounds of golf. You've sown into our hearts with wisdom, grace, and patience. (Ahoy!)

To **Aunt Loretta**—you've been by my side since the beginning of my salvation journey. You calmed me down when I thought Y2K was the end of the world, and you've been smiling, listening, and praying ever since. Thank you for being a safe place.

To my pastors, **JJ and Trina Hairston**—thank you for leading with vulnerability and truth. Your willingness to share your own journey has given me and so many others the courage to believe for victory in our own marriages. Great leaders lead by example, and yours is one worth following.

And last, but never least—to **my Daddy**—you are the best father I could have ever asked for. Thank you for baptizing me at eight years old, and for praying for me long before I ever arrived.

Thank you for loving me, guiding me, and for sparing me from names like *Christmas Dae* or *Cinnamon Danish*. I don't think anyone would have taken me seriously as an author with names like those—but I know you meant well.

I love you, Papa. Forever.

About the Author

Capri Lee is a devoted wife, mother, and intercessor with a passion for helping others find God in the middle of life's most complex and painful moments. Since marrying Kevin Lee, Sr. in May 2013 and welcoming their son KJ in March 2023, Capri has leaned deeply into her relationship with Christ to navigate the challenges and joys of family life.

She is a woman shaped by grace—healed through the loss of her mother and cousin, restored through marital struggles, and strengthened through surrender. Her writing reflects a heart that is transparent, tender, and transformed.

Capri began her walk with God as a young girl kneeling alone in quiet faith—and today, she writes to encourage others not to cast away their confidence. Through every moment of confusion, neglect, grief, and growth, she has discovered that God truly gives purpose to our pain.

This is her debut devotional, born not from perfection but from a surrendered heart that chose to believe that God will save her husband.

Follow Capri Lee:

- Facebook: Capri Lee

- Instagram: @capri.d.lee

www.ingramcontent.com/pod-product-compliance
Lightning Source LLC
LaVergne TN
LVHW020716110826
845149LV00012B/2292